THE APARTMENT FARMER

THE HASSLE-FREE WAY TO GROW VEGETABLES INDOORS, ON BALCONIES, PATIOS, ROOFS, AND IN SMALL YARDS

BY DUANE NEWCOMB

Published by J.P. Tarcher, Inc., Los Angeles

Distributed by Hawthorn Books, Inc., New York

Library of Congress Catalog Card Number: 75-27972

ISBN (softcover): 0-87477-047-5
ISBN (hardcover): 0-87477-045-9

Manufactured in the United States of America

Illustrations by The Committee and by Barbara Brody

Typesetting by Freedmen's Organization

Published by J. P. Tarcher, Inc.
9110 Sunset Blvd., Los Angeles, California 90069

Published simultaneously in Canada by
Prentice-Hall of Canada, Ltd.
1870 Birchmount Road, Scarborough, Ontario

1 2 3 4 5 6 7 8 9 0

Table of Contents

The Promise of Apartment Farming

The only way you can grow a good crop of vegetables—I mean a really good crop—is outside in the sun in the ground, right? That's what I used to think, until one day an apartment-dweller friend came by, took a look at my outdoor garden (which I think is pretty successful), and snorted, "My beans and tomatoes can beat yours leaves down."

Well, a couple of days later I dropped by his place, and with a smirk asked to see his garden.

I was absolutely amazed. He had a veritable farm in his flat.

Radishes, lettuce, beets, carrots, and more grew in splendid profusion on five windowsills. Beans formed a giant curtain on the outside of several windows. Herbs grew under lights set up in various rooms. On the patio tomatoes hung in containers under the eaves, and corn and watermelon grew in half whiskey-barrels on the deck. (There are people who'd argue emptying the barrel is more fun than filling it, but anyway . . .)

"How's this for a strawberry?" my friend said, plucking one out of a pot. I popped it in my mouth. My friends, I swear to you, I had just eaten the king of all strawberries.

After that I couldn't wait to get home and give it a try. First, I started growing salad vegetables and herbs on windowsill shelves. Then I planted corn and other larger crops in containers on the patio. From there I went wild and began collecting gourmet and exotic vegetables that I thought would

1

do well in limited space . . . things like serpent cucumbers and white eggplant and even something called vegetable spaghetti.

After that I started to look for unusual ways to apartment-farm, and in the process discovered many new methods and lots of unusual research that makes indoor gardening a real delight.

And that's what this book is about: how to farm your apartment. Or your patio, balcony, or rooftop. We will show you how literally to farm your indoors by successfully growing vegetables under lights. In essence, we will turn you into a "closet farmer."

We will look at vegetables and herbs especially useful to the gourmet cook, at "show-off" vegetables that are conversation pieces or will otherwise dress up your apartment, and at midget vegetables that get the most mileage out of your soil.

Here, then, is the promise of apartment farming.

• *It is not messy, troublesome, or difficult.* It need not make your apartment ugly looking. It need not endanger your place with leaks, dry rot, bugs, and smells.

• *You can grow vegetables almost anywhere.* They will thrive in apartment or home garden spots that you'd normally ignore: between balcony railings, on the stairs, under the eaves in hanging pots, in converted bookcases on the patio, on A-frames in the bedroom. You *can't* grow endless salads in a half dozen 6-inch pots, of course, but then you're not just raising plants to eat—you're raising them for the pleasure of seeing them grow, watching the leaves appear, the flower buds turn into tomatoes, and feeling a part of the wonder of nature day by day as your vegetables ripen.

• *It is easier than farming outdoors.* Growing vegetables in an apartment or other limited space is much simpler than trying to battle the elements outdoors. You can even garden in your pajamas. The techniques in this book stress easy-to-follow watering, fertilizing, and planting concepts that make container vegetable gardening practically foolproof. For instance, we give you *one* soil mix that does everything.

• *You can grow specialty vegetables that are difficult to buy.* If you have trouble obtaining cress, escarole, fennel, salsify, purslane, special Oriental or other gourmet foods and herbs, you can order them from seed catalogs and grow them yourself. We tell you where to go to get them.

• *You can garden with kitchen utensils.* Except for a trowel or small shovel, the only tools you need are already in your kitchen—measuring cups, mixing bowls, and so on. Just think—you can cook eggplant parmigiana while you're growing it!

•*It doesn't cost a lot of money.* No fancy fertilizers, tools, or containers are needed.

And that's what apartment farming is all about. For people who are already into indoor plants, container vegetable gardening opens a whole new window for their experience (being careful not to let in a draft on the seedlings). You can convert those pots and containers you already have to something that is not only beautiful but edible.

And one of the nicest things about apartment farming is that you also don't need any experience at all, and as you go along, this book will take you step by step, giving you all the information you need to be successful.

There's one piece of wisdom that my indoor farming friend imparted to me which I wrote down very carefully, word for word. The truth of this statement is so unmistakable that its inspirational value never fails. "Keep in mind," he said, "that if you don't tell your carrots where they are growing, nobody will."

Now, start growing those indoor carrots, radishes, tomatoes, and cukes. And remember, "Shhhh."

CHAPTER TWO

Discovering the Space

I don't think I've ever met apartment dwellers who weren't convinced they weren't already utilizing every inch available. In fact, most complain their places are already so crowded—with furniture, house plants, art objects, and the like—that they couldn't possibly find room to grow a lot of vegetables.

But are they really that crowded? The pleasant fact is that no matter how jam-packed your apartment or living space is, you almost *always* have a great deal of growing area that you've simply overlooked. Take one small step for mankind and you might just be taking one giant step for a beet.

Consider how much space you need for an apartment garden. If you have ten 8-inch pots, you can grow:
—80 carrots,
—40 beets, and
—40 or more cherry tomatoes.

If you have separate 5- or 10-gallon containers, you can also grow 60 zucchini, 30 or 40 cucumbers, and 12 ears of corn.

And this size garden can easily be squeezed into a corner of a patio or balcony. Or grown indoors on a windowsill in combination with a small outdoor window box. You can nearly *always* find this much space in any apartment.

You can't plan your apartment farm until you've found out exactly how much space you have available to grow vegetables in. As a first step, divide your apartment into three distinct growing areas:

1. windowsill space,
2. patio/balcony/rooftop area,
3. indoor apartment space (for growing vegetables under lights).

Measure the length of all apartment windowsills in feet. Three windows, each with a 4-foot sill, will net you 12 feet of growing space. This will allow you to grow a wide variety of vegetables in eighteen 6-inch pots (or 4-inch ones, in some cases). A young indoor gardener I know says she's grown seven kinds of herbs, beets, lettuce, tomatoes, and a lot more on the sill of just three windows. In addition, her plants know no season and she harvests many kinds of vegetables all winter long.

See the three Apartment Farmer Windowsill Gardens described below and on following pages.

**Indoor Farming
Your Windowsill**

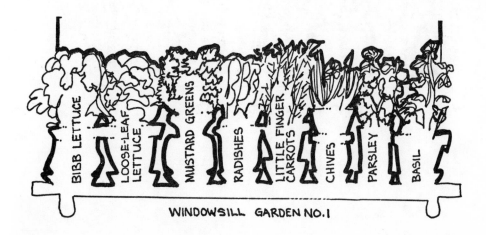

BIBB LETTUCE LOOSE-LEAF LETTUCE MUSTARD GREENS RADISHES LITTLE FINGER CARROTS CHIVES PARSLEY BASIL

WINDOWSILL GARDEN NO. 1

TINY TIM TOMATOES

BURPEE'S PIXIE HYBRID TOMATOES

BURPEE'S PIXIE HYBRID TOMATOES

PRESTO HYBRID TOMATOES

BEETS

BEETS

GREEN ONIONS

GREEN ONIONS

CHIVES

BASIL

ROSEMARY

PARSLEY

BIBB LETTUCE

LOOSE-LEAF LETTUCE

SPINACH

SPINACH

SPINACH

LITTLE FINGER CARROTS

LITTLE FINGER CARROTS

RADISHES

WINDOWSILL GARDEN NO. 2

6

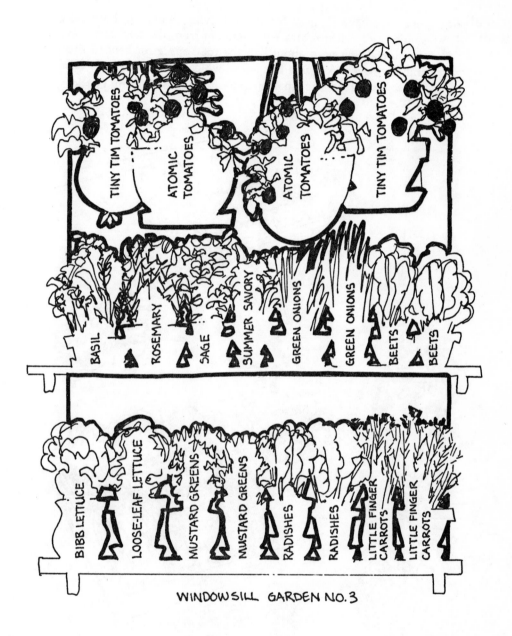

WINDOWSILL GARDEN NO. 3

Outdoor Farming Your Windowbox, Balcony, Patio, or Rooftop

Measure the entire balcony (patio, rooftop) space first. A 9-by-15-foot balcony, for instance, contains 135 square feet. Next estimate how much space you'll need for general living, lounging, barbecuing, and similar uses. Then subtract this amount from the total space available. If you feel you need about half the total space for general living, you still have over 65 square feet left in which to cultivate your farm.

See the three basic Apartment Farmer Patio/Balcony Gardens, pages 8-10.

OUTDOOR GARDEN NO. 1

OUTDOOR GARDEN NO. 2

9

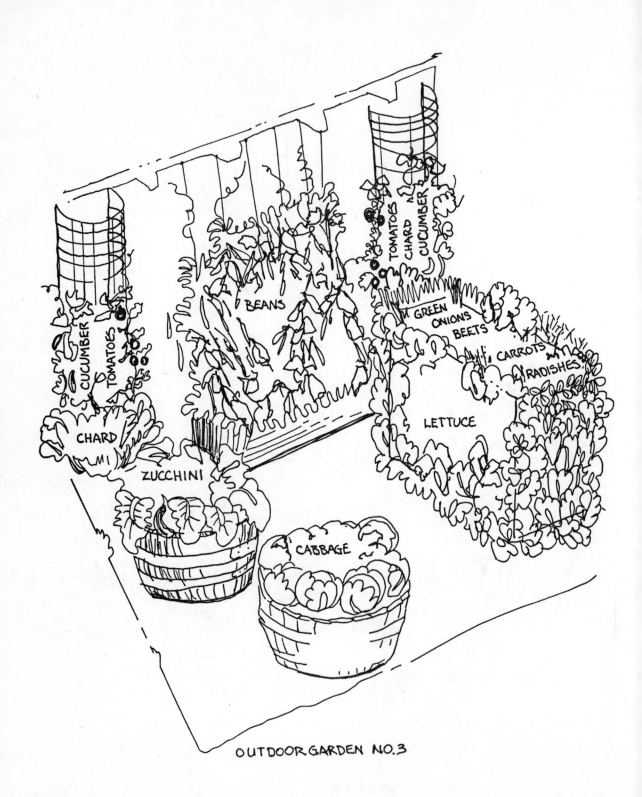

CUCUMBER
TOMATOES
CHARD
MI
ZUCCHINI
BEANS
TOMATOES
CHARD
CUCUMBER
GREEN
ONIONS
BEETS
CARROTS
RADISHES
LETTUCE
CABBAGE

OUTDOOR GARDEN NO. 3

10

First sketch your layout, including the bedrooms, kitchen, living room, closets, bathroom, and any additional interior space. Now walk through each of these rooms and look for unused space where you might grow vegetables under lights, either on wall-shelf units or free-standing vertical fixtures (being careful not to bump into your mate, whom you might want to replace with a rutabaga).

See the three basic Apartment Farmer Light Gardens, pages 11-13.

Indoor Farming Your Bedroom (or Closet, Attic, or Basement) with Artificial Lights

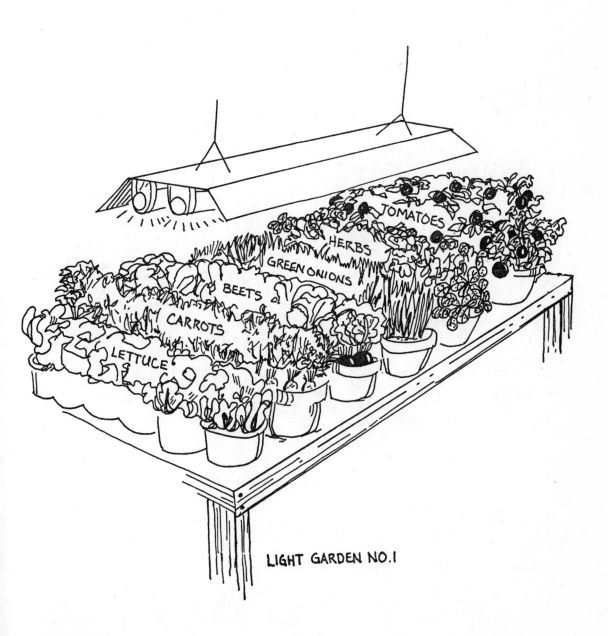

LIGHT GARDEN NO. 1

LIGHT GARDEN NO. 2

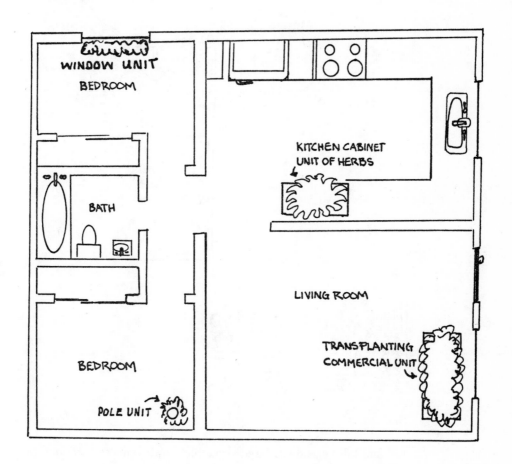

WINDOW UNIT

BEDROOM

BATH

KITCHEN CABINET
UNIT OF HERBS

LIVING ROOM

BEDROOM

POLE UNIT

TRANSPLANTING
COMMERCIAL UNIT

LIGHT GARDEN NO. 3

**The Best Places
to Grow What**

Where you put your farm depends on the space available and on your preferences. There are, however, four rules you'll want to consider when you think about planting:

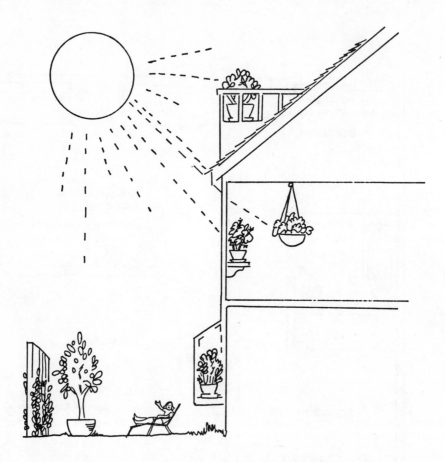

1. Plant tall vegetables, large vegetables, and climbers outdoors.
2. Make sure vegetables that produce fruits (such as tomatoes, cucumbers, and eggplant) receive six hours of direct sun a day, either indoors or out. (On rainy days let them watch television.)
3. Place herbs in full sun (five hours minimum), either indoors or outdoors.
4. Place root and leafy vegetables where it's possible to obtain 1,000 foot-candles of light; that is, about six to eight hours of light a day. That's the equivalent of being outdoors in a semi-shady location or indoors under two standard 40-watt fluorescent fixtures positioned 3 inches away from the plant for 12 to 14 hours a day.

Outdoors on a patio, balcony, rooftop, or in a window box you can grow beans, broccoli, Brussels sprouts, cabbage, cantaloupe, cucumber, peppers, potatoes, squash, herbs, and most root and leafy vegetables.

Indoors on a windowsill you can grow carrots, cress, herbs, lettuce, mustard greens, radishes, spinach, sprouts, tomatoes, and zucchini.

Indoors under lights you can grow beets, carrots, celery, Chinese cabbage, cucumber, endive, herbs, lettuce, onions (green), parsley, radishes, sprouts, tomatoes, watercress.

How to Find Space You Didn't Dream You Could Use

The important thing to realize is that by utilizing *vertical space*—hanging-basket space, extra shelves, and other methods we'll take up later—you can double, even triple, the available garden space in all apartment areas.

Finding apartment gardening space may take some three-dimensional thinking, for you can garden not only the two-dimensional floor area but much of the vertical space as well. Don't confine yourself to a few containers sitting on the floor. Try growing vegetables in hanging containers under the eaves, in vertical floor-to-ceiling vegetable gardens made of chicken wire, sphagnum moss, and plywood, or in A-frame containers placed in the middle of the patio area. (We will discuss the details of building these containers in Chapter 6.)

Under lights you can construct an A-frame vegetable garden, build a complete garden in a kitchen cabinet, and more.

A good deal more about structures and containers is given in Chapters 5, 6, and 7.

In finding garden space, look for the following:

Outdoors
—Places to hang containers—for example, under the eaves or in the middle of the patio.
—Space against the wall in which to construct vertical container gardens.
—Places to put special free-standing vertical structures, such as roll-around vegetable cases, floor-to-ceiling pole trees, A-frame raised gardens.
—Outside space for extended window boxes.

Around Windows
—Space for additional shelves across windows.
—Room for hanging containers in windows.
—Windowsills that can be made 6 or more inches wide.
—Extended window space in which to put a modified window-box greenhouse.
—Windows in which you can place floor-to-ceiling vertical containers.

—Unused tops of tables, bureaus, cabinets, and similar structures.
—Unused wall space a foot or more wide in any room.
—Empty shelves in bookcases, cabinets, closets, and storage areas.
—Unused indoor areas suitable for small, vertical fluorescent fixtures.

How to Plan Your Apartment Farm

These preliminaries completed, now consider your vegetable needs, your living habits, desires, amount of space available, and so on. Ask yourself these questions:

—What quantities of vegetables do I want—large, moderate, or small?

—Do I want to grow specialized crops such as herbs, sprouts, or gourmet vegetables?

—How much living area do I want to farm?

—How much experimenting do I want to do with unusual ways of growing vegetables, such as having vertical hanging gardens or growing vegetables under lights?

—Do I want my vegetables to be decorative or simply utilitarian?

Don't worry about getting every square inch planted to begin with. You can start off utilizing only the most desirable space and go (or grow) from there. Mistakes will inevitably be made, and so having spare room left in which to move things around is desirable.

Now make a rough sketch of your apartment. Then, with the answers to the above questions in mind, lay out generally where you intend to put your apartment farm, indicating more or less the vegetables you'd like to grow and the type of containers you intend to use. If necessary, read Chapters 5, 6, and 7 first, then come back and complete your planning.

Here are three examples.

Example 1. Suppose you have 15 square feet of patio space, 15 square feet of window space, and 30 square feet of possible indoor gardening room. You want to grow a wide variety of vegetables (including corn and beans) but in moderate quantities, and you want to grow them in a utilitarian manner in limited space away from your living area. Since corn and beans generally require outdoor space (with some exceptions, which we'll go into later), and since you want moderate quantities grown in limited space away from the living area, you should grow vegetables in four or five conventional containers (whiskey-barrel halves, for instance) in a corner of the patio.

Example 2. On the other hand, suppose you don't have outdoor space, you want to grow a few vegetables and herbs for salads, you want them out of the way, and you want simple gardening. You have a choice of growing vegetables on the windowsill or under lights. Since you want simple gardening, you should probably limit yourself to a half-dozen or so pots on the windowsill.

Example 3. Suppose you have balcony space, a good-sized windowsill area, and plenty of interior space, and you want to live with your garden and innovate in as decorative a way as possible. This indicates you should garden all areas. In addition, you will want to go all out with hanging containers, vertical patio gardens, and other unusual planting methods that will fit your decor.

Apartment farming, then, offers tremendous versatility and will fit any lifestyle and every possible kind of apartment combination. Now let's start putting your farm together.

CHAPTER THREE

Getting Started

The great thing about apartment farming is that you can garden in almost any type of container. If you want to, you can have fun with decorator-type containers—antique stoves, off-beat bowls, tubs, kettles, dishpans, wastebaskets, cookie jars, picnic baskets, ice chests, and so on.

Or, you can improvise with other available materials (after all, plants don't really care what kind of containers they grow in), such as clay pots, plastic pots, paper pots, Styrofoam pots, milk cartons, ice cream cartons, coffee cans, bleach containers, cut-off wine bottles, plastic bags, and raised beds lined with black plastic. (Just think—you might wind up sleeping in your lettuce patch.)

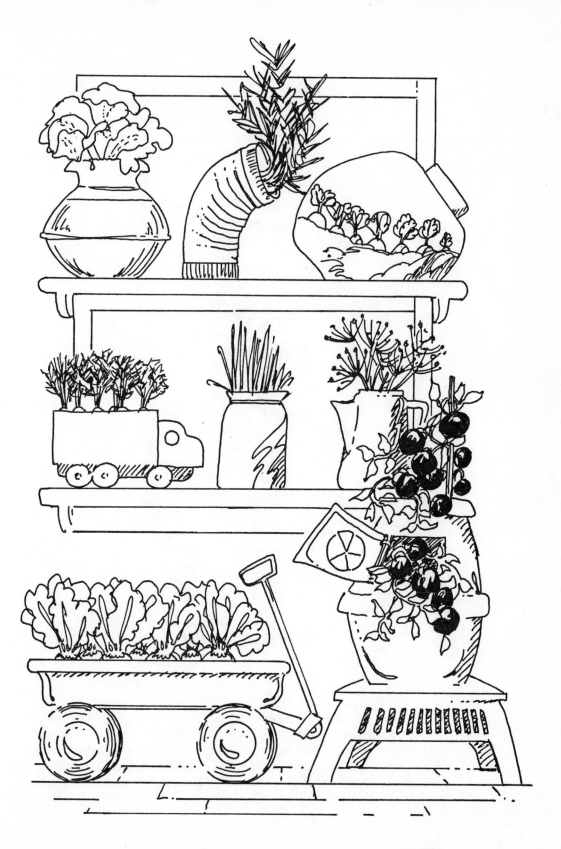

19

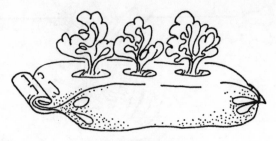

PLASTIC BAG

WHISKEY-BARREL HALF

You can use large containers such as redwood planter boxes and other wooden boxes (coat the insides with asphalt paint to prevent rot), plastic garbage cans (line with plastic, fill with soil, punch holes for both plants and drainage), chicken-wire containers (line with black plastic), and wine-barrel or whiskey-barrel halves.

For continuing reference the following chart will give you a good idea of the sizes and capacities of several kinds of containers.

Container	Approximate soil capacity
Clay pots (diameter)	
4 in.	2½ cups
6 in.	2½ qt.
8 in.	1 gal.
10 in.	2¼ gal.
12 in.	3½ gal.
14 in.	6 gal.
Two-pound coffee can	½ gal.
Milk cartons	½ gal.
	1 gal.
Wastebasket	3 gal.
Large ice cream carton	5 gal.
Garbage cans	10 gal.
	20 gal.
	30 gal.
Whiskey-barrel half	15 gal.

Generally, the larger and deeper the container, the better the yields. However, size doesn't matter much if you can provide a soil depth of at least 8 inches. Individual vegetables have very specific soil requirements (which we will tell you about). While you can grow cherry tomatoes (the little red ones) in smaller containers, the large varieties require up to 20 gallons (3 cubic feet) of soil to produce a good crop.

The kind of container you get will determine the amount of watering you will do, since some materials are better than others at holding water without evaporation. Wooden containers hold moisture well and need less watering than clay pots. Styrofoam pots also require less watering than clay. Nonporous containers such as stoneware, glass, ceramic, and plastic do not need as frequent watering as do most other materials. All, however, need drain holes.

Remember, if you don't like the looks of plastic or Styrofoam, you can always put it *inside* a nice-looking wooden, clay, wicker, or whatever container.

Do you have to prepare the containers? Yes, a little. For wooden containers, you should either drill holes in the bottom (and put a pan underneath to catch the water) or place a 2-inch layer of coarse gravel in the bottom before adding soil. Treat the inside of wood containers with a nontoxic wood preservative or asphalt paint. For plastic containers and tin cans, punch holes on the *sides* (not the bottom), about ½ inch above the bottom. Do not bore holes in the bottom of any plastic container, since this often weakens the base too much for the weight of the soil.

As a general overall rule, containers less than 10 inches in diameter need a hole ½ inch in diameter to provide good drainage. Containers over 10 inches in diameter need two to four holes.

Two cautions here: When utilizing old containers (those that have already grown a crop), scrub them with a vegetable brush in soapy water, then rinse them in boiling water. This prevents disease organisms from being carried over to the next crop.

Always place saucers, foil pans, or trays under containers if there is any chance of water stain on floors, furniture, or windowsills.

Prior to planting, place shards or gravel in bottom of your planting container. This will promote drainage and hold in the potting soil.

You can easily carry smaller containers from place to place, but the larger containers full of soil are much too heavy to move easily. Consider these methods to increase mobility: Equip tubs, whiskey-barrel

halves, and large wooden containers with casters; place three or four large containers on a child's wagon: move large containers on a small throw rug.

Additional container material is given in later chapters that apply specifically to growing vegetables on windowsills, patios, and under lights.

The great thing about apartment farming is that if you grow indoors under lights or on the windowsill, you can plant many vegetables almost any time of the year. You create your own microclimate that knows no season.

Inside, all plants seem to grow satisfactorily at about 70 degrees. (Most apartments are generally kept at 68 to 75 degrees.) It is possible, however, to achieve greater growth for some plants by varying the temperature slightly. Consider, for instance, closing off one room to keep it somewhat cooler than the rest of the house.

Planting outside in window boxes or in patio or balcony containers, of course, subjects you to somewhat the same kind of schedule as outdoor gardening.

The main factor in determining when to plant, both indoors and out, is temperature. Vegetables are basically divided into warm season and cool season crops.

Warm Season Plants. These are harvested for fruit—the part of the plant with the seeds—such as tomatoes, peppers, eggplant, beans, melons, and pumpkins. They need quite a bit of heat and fairly long days. Generally, the average daytime temperature must rise over 65 degrees for any of these plants to do well. For instance, I've planted tomatoes on the patio in April and had them do almost nothing till the first of May, when the days begin to warm up. In some cases, I've planted tomatoes a month apart and had the last one planted mature first, simply because it wasn't set back by the cold days.

Cool Season Plants. These do well in cool weather—generally between 45 degrees and 65 degrees. They are the leafy and root vegetables, such as beets, carrots, cabbage, spinach, lettuce, and broccoli. (Peas also are a cool season plant, even if we harvest the fruit.) During the cool days these plants expend all their energy forming leafy and root materials. When the days warm up (usually over 65 degrees), they put their energy into producing seed.

Here is a temperature-range chart that will help you in growing vegetables indoors.

Cool Season and Warm Season Crops

Cool season crops—adapted to 45° to 65°F.:

Tolerant of some frost: asparagus, beets, broccoli, Brussels Sprouts, cabbage, kale, mustard greens, New Zealand spinach, onions, radishes, spinach, turnips and rutabagas.

Intolerant of frost at maturity: carrots, cauliflower, endive, lettuce, peas, rhubarb, Swiss chard.

Warm season crops—requiring 65° to 80° F. day and night (and readily damaged by frost):

Beans, corn, cucumbers, eggplant, melons, okra, peppers, squash, tomatoes.

Besides warm season and cool season vegetables, we also have early and later varieties. The early varieties require less heat to mature than do the later varieties. If you live in an area that is cool until late spring (the northernmost states, for instance) and then has a short summer, you should consider an earlier variety. In addition, you can use this early-, mid- and late-maturing quality of vegetables to stretch out the season.

All this means is that you must watch the heat requirements of particular plants to know when to plant in your area. You can estimate this by using the frost map included here. This will give you a general guide, although there may be many different microclimates within each region, so geographical points only a few miles apart may vary as to the date of the last killing frost by as much as ten to fifteen days. For more precision, check your newspaper weather forecasts.

Pick out your zone on the map and determine the average date of the last killing frost. The planting list, below, will tell you approximately on what date to plant particular vegetables. For instance, if you live in Zone 3, the average dates of the last killing frost occur between May 1 and May 15. Referring to the planting list, you will find you can plant broccoli sometime between April 1 and April 15, beets between May 1 and May 15, and tomatoes and corn after May 15, when the ground in your patio containers has warmed up.

Planting with a Frost Map

1. In Zones 6, 7, 8, and 9, plant these vegetables from fall to early spring. In all other zones plant these vegetables 2 to 4 weeks before the last killing frost in spring:

   broccoli — Brussels sprouts — kale — lettuce — mustard greens — onions — peas — radishes — rutabagas — turnips

2. Plant these vegetables on approximately the date of the last frost. They tolerate cool weather and very light frost:

   beets — cabbage — carrots — cauliflower — Swiss chard

3. Plant these vegetables after the ground has warmed up:

   beans — corn — cucumbers — eggplant — melons — okra — peppers — squash — tomatoes

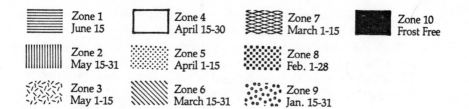

Zone 1 June 15		Zone 4 April 15-30		Zone 7 March 1-15		Zone 10 Frost Free	
Zone 2 May 15-31		Zone 5 April 1-15		Zone 8 Feb. 1-28			
Zone 3 May 1-15		Zone 6 March 15-31		Zone 9 Jan. 15-31			

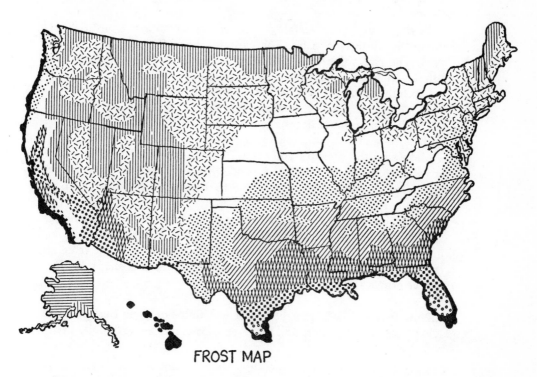

FROST MAP

If you intend to plant fairly standard vegetables, you will probably want to buy your seed from a rack because it gives you a chance to browse and compare. We are, without a doubt, in the grip of the greatest vegetable boom this country has ever known. As a result, every spring seed racks offer a cornucopia of vegetables.

If you're looking for novelties, mini-vegetables, and unusual gourmet vegetables, however, you'll probably have to buy your seed through a catalog. Go through the catalog list at the back of this book (Appendix A) and send for several. As we mention various vegetables, we will indicate which firms offer that particular specialty.

Buying from Seed Racks. Seed racks usually contain varieties that perform well in your area, but companies often include varieties with a national reputation that may not adapt well to your conditions. If

How to Buy Vegetables from Seed Racks and Catalogs

you're in doubt about which variety to plant for outdoor use, check your local nursery before making a selection.

Check the seed package expiration dates. Companies usually change the seed seasonally, but in some cases old seed may stay on a rack. The date is your guarantee that the seed is fresh and viable. In addition, some seed, such as onion, are short-lived and need to be planted as soon as possible.

Buying from Seed Catalogs. Order with caution from regional companies in distant states. The varieties they offer may not fit your area. The real value of a catalog is that a particular company often offers varieties available from no other source.

Carefully check the number of days to maturity. Order "early-to-harvest" varieties where summers are short, as in the northernmost states. In hot summer areas, you can stretch the season by planting both early- and late-maturing varieties.

Make sure the varieties you grow fit your growing space. If you're growing tomatoes in small pots inside, or under limited patio conditions, for instance, you may want to consider the tomatoes bred especially for small containers, such as Tiny Tim, Burpee Pixie Hybrid, Presto Hybrid, Patio Hybrid, and Small Fry. (More about this later.)

Give consideration to the aesthetic and novelty effects you want. For instance, just for fun you can grow radish varieties that range from all red to half red to full white, and if you can hybridize a shade of blue, you've grown the first Bicentennial Radish.

Now that you've gotten your feet wet (but not your rug), let's see what kind of soil, water, and fertilizer your container vegetables need.

CHAPTER FOUR

Soil, Water, Planting, and Other Considerations

Apartment farming can magically transform a bleak, drab apartment or other living space into a virtual Garden of Eden. However, apartment dwellers often have trouble visualizing the delicious results of their labors and instead have all sorts of apprehensions. The soil is too heavy to carry upstairs. Gardening is too messy to do indoors. Bugs will invade the apartment. Water will ruin the rugs. You can't leave plants alone over the weekend. Temperature and light present problems.

If this is where you are, hold it right there. This book is not just about gardening brought indoors; it gives you a complete *system* for solving the problems of indoor gardening—easily and simply.

Let's start with the "soil" you are going to use.

Container Soil for Apartment Farming

Some indoor gardeners simply go out and dig up common garden soil in which to grow vegetables. In a contained space, however, soil becomes compacted much more easily than it does in the ground. It dries out faster, or in some cases drains poorly, creating a root-rot problem. It is best, therefore, to use a special container soil for vegetable gardening.

A good potting mix is a combination of organic material (bark, compost, peat moss) and minerals (soil, sand, vermiculite, and other ingredients). It must provide the right nutrients for vegetable growth and enough air space (despite container compacting) to allow good air and water movement.

Actually, it is possible to grow vegetables in "soilless" mixes (the commercial potting mixes). I find, however, that vegetables do much better in a combination of soil, potting mix, and other ingredients. These soil mixes require less frequent feeding than does a potting mix alone, and a combination soil-potting mix holds water better. Now, here's a soil mix that grows all vegetables well:

The All-Purpose Apartment Farmer Soil Mix

½ gallon each of:

    Commercial potting mix
    Compost (homemade or purchased) or vermiculite
    Common garden soil

These three easily obtained ingredients and the mixing instructions that follow are all you need to begin your farm.

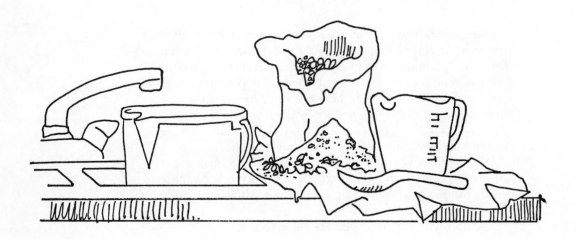

No-Mess Mixing Techniques

Needed implements are: a 5-gallon plastic pail, 1-quart kitchen measuring cup, large wooden spoon, plastic sheet or oil cloth to put over your kitchen work area to catch spillage.

Mix the ingredients above in the plastic pail in the kitchen sink. Moisten the contents with hot water to cut down on the dust. Stir slowly with a wooden spoon until everything is mixed.

If you're mixing large quantities, pour the ingredients together in a big can or on a piece of plastic. Moisten them with hot water to keep down the dust. Don't try to stir, but pick up a little of the ingredients in a dustpan and deposit them in another spot to create a new pile. Repeat this until the ingredients become completely mixed.

Now let's take a quick look at what's in our all-purpose soil mix.

Commercial Potting Mix. Many synthetic commercial potting mixes contain all the ingredients necessary for good plant growth. The most popular of these mixes were perfected at Cornell University and the University of California. You can buy modified mixes under the names Jiffy Mix, Pro Mix, and Redi Earth. The University of California formula is available under the names First Step and Super Soil.

If you'd rather make your own potting mix, here's the formula for the Cornell mix, and coming from an Ivy League college you *know* it's got to be good.

vermiculite	8 quarts
shredded peat moss	8 quarts
superphosphate	2 level tablespoons
limestone	2 tablespoons
dried cow manure or steamed bone meal	8 tablespoons

Measure and place all ingredients in the garbage can liner. Shake vigorously.

Since the Cornell mix has no smell, you can place it in plastic bags and store in the back of a closet, being careful not to get any dirt on your shoes.

Vermiculite. This is mineral mica expanded by high heat. It holds moisture for long periods of time. You can buy it from any nursery or garden center.

Common Garden Soil (Loam). Soil should contain both organic material and mineral matter and should have a soil structure that allows free movement of air and water. An ideal soil for plant growth contains about 50 percent solid matter and 50 percent air space. To find good rich loam, select your soil from a garden area that is already growing vigorously. Even if you live in the city and can't just go out to the park and dig up what you want (chances are that soil wouldn't be great anyway), you can buy top soil from a nursery or florist (or beg some off your suburban friends).

Purchased soil is already sterilized. Soil from the ground is not and you might want to sterilize to destroy weed seed and nematodes (a small microscopic worm) and to avoid passing on fungus diseases, particularly something called damping off, which causes the seedlings to shrivel just above the soil level.

You can sterilize your soil by spreading it out in a shallow pan and baking it at 275 degrees for an hour. To overcome the problem of odor, soak the soil thoroughly before putting it in the oven.

For myself, I use the soil without baking and take my chances with the potential problems mentioned above, since I do not want to destroy the useful bacteria. It's one of those garden trade-offs, and every gardener can decide for himself how he wants to handle it.

How to Plant Seeds

You can sow most seeds directly into containers, especially if you intend to grow those vegetables indoors. Bush beans, beets, carrots, peas, radishes, rutabagas, spinach, and turnips should be planted directly, since they don't transplant well. Most others you can start from seed in one container, then transplant to another later. (Generally, this gives you a head start on the outdoor gardening season.)

The way to seed directly is as follows:

1. Soak the soil thoroughly before planting.
2. Space the seed across the container according to the directions on the seed package—or see the instructions for intercropping near the end of this chapter.
3. Cover the seed with some container soil. Different vegetable seeds require different planting depths. Specific instructions for each vegetable are given in Chapter 8.

Starting Seeds Indoors in Containers

Much of the fun of apartment farming comes from planting your own seeds indoors, whether on your windowsill or under lights. There are two fairly easy methods. Ideally, once the seedlings have emerged, you should give them about 12 hours a day of sunlight or place them 6 inches below two 40-watt fluorescent tubes burning up to 14 hours a day. If you can't manage the ideal conditions, come as close as you can. Unless you're terribly far off, the seedling will come up anyway.

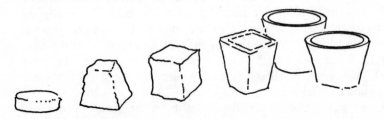

BIODEGRADABLE POTS AND CUBES

The One-Step Method: No Repotting. With this technique you sow seeds directly into small pots or cubes made of biodegradable material that are placed directly into the final container and left there. The roots grow through the material into the soil in the pots. This procedure allows the plant to avoid root shock on transplanting. There are five kinds of pots or cubes readily available.

1. *Jiffy 7 Pellets* are compressed pellets made of sterile sphagnum peat and soil with added fertilizer. The pellet expands to make a small container when it is placed in water. Place the seed directly in the compressed peat pot and plant the entire container.
2. *BR 8 Blocks* are fiber blocks containing fertilizer. After the plant has reached the desired size, the blocks are planted in the final container.
3. *Kys Kubes* are fiber cubes containing fertilizer. Plant the entire cube.
4. *Fertl-cubes* are made from a blend of mosses, plant food, and vermiculite. Each cube has a depression for planting seed. Place both cube and plant directly in the final container.
5. *Peat Pots* are fiber pots that you are supposed to fill with synthetic soil. Plant the entire pot directly in the larger container.

Here's how to plant: Thoroughly water the small pot or cube and sow seeds two at a time directly into it. Insert the cubes in a small plastic bag and set them in a warm space. Remove the bag after the seedlings have appeared. Plant in their final container whenever the seedlings reach 2 to 6 inches high.

ONE-STEP METHOD

The Two-Step Method: Repotting. Fill several aluminum bread pans, frozen food pans, or meat loaf pans, with vermiculite. (Half-gallon milk

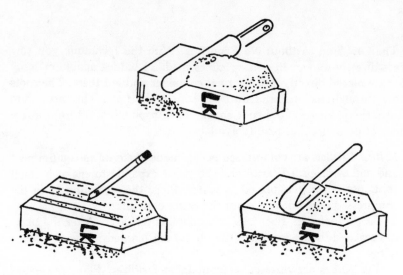

BEGINNING OF TWO-STEP METHOD

cartons cut in half lengthwise or 1-gallon bleach containers cut off 3 inches above the bottom also make good containers.) Make sure you punch a few drain holes along the sides to let the water in (see below). Scrape off excess vermiculite with a flat knife and press the remaining vermiculite down firmly with a solid spatula.

—Make seed furrows about 2 inches apart with a pencil.

—Sow seeds directly from the seed package about 1 inch apart. Sow more seeds than the number of plants needed; then when they come up, thin out the weaker plants and leave the stronger ones for transplanting. You can thin easily by simply clipping the plants off with a small pair of scissors.

—Cover the seeds with vermiculite.

—Water from the bottom. Put 1 or 2 inches of water in the bottom of the kitchen sink and place the seed container in it. When the surface of the vermiculite becomes moist (touch it to see), take the container out and allow it to drain.

—Slip the trays into a plastic bag (a bread bag will do fine) and keep as close to 75 degrees as possible. Don't water again until after germination, and after that add only enough water to keep the vermiculite damp.

A caution here: Too much water can interfere with germination. If mildew appears because the container is too moist, take the cover off and let it dry out.

If seedlings do not show up right away, be patient. Most seeds take five to fifteen days to germinate. If, however, you think they are taking too long, dig up one or two seeds with the prong of a kitchen fork and check for new growth. If there is none, replant.

—When the first true leaves have formed (the second pair you'll see), carefully dig the seedlings out and put them into 3- or 4-inch peat or plastic pots filled with soil mix. (The first plant parts that you'll see are cotyledons, food storage containers. True leaves don't come until later and are the first parts out of the ground that really look like leaves.) The easiest way to do your transplanting (and not injure the roots) is to break the soil an inch from, and all around, the young plant with a kitchen fork. If you are using a foil pan, you can simply cut the pan apart with a pair of scissors and lift the plants out with a spatula. When you transplant, make sure the seed leaves are about a half inch above the top of the soil. Put the pots on a tray and insert in a plastic bag.

—Transfer from there directly into the final container.

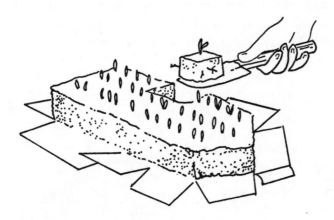

Some vegetables—such as Brussels sprouts, broccoli, cabbage, cauliflower, eggplant, peppers, and tomatoes—seem to get off to a better start if they are first grown from seed indoors and then later

Buying Seedlings and Transplanting

33

transplanted as seedlings. Actually, this is *easier* than buying seeds, since you start with larger plants. In general, transplants have a head start—especially if you're planting a patio, since they're already well developed by the time it's warm enough to plant outdoors. It's also fun to shop the nurseries when you can pick out 4- to 10-inch plants to pop into your containers. Usually a tremendous selection of vegetables is available during early spring months; after that it becomes more difficult to find what you want.

The procedure for transplanting seedlings is really fairly simple.

—Make sure the spacing between seedlings is correct (see table, opposite page).

—Dig a hole in your soil mix with a large kitchen spoon, making the hole big enough to avoid bending or squeezing the root mass.

—Place the plant in the hole, trying not to disturb the roots any more than necessary.

—Bury the roots at least 1 inch below the surface. This prevents the plant from falling over easily. Simply hold the seedling in the hole with your right hand; then, with the spoon, fill around the roots and push the soil back.

(I told you it was fairly simple.)

Spacing for Container Plants

If you plan to plant young seedlings in outdoor containers, you should get them used to outdoor conditions. Begin by taking them out in the morning, then at night, if there is any frost danger, bring them indoors. Gradually expose them to low temperatures and more sunlight for about two weeks until you can leave them out without damage.

When planting the seeds, you need not space them any particular distance apart. Simply scatter them across the entire container rather than in rows. Later, however, you should thin the seedlings.

Carrots, for instance, are thinned first to ¾ inch apart, then to 1 to 2 inches (it is expected you will eat the small carrots), radishes are thinned to 1 inch apart. Two 8-inch containers of carrots planted on a 1-inch spacing will produce the equivalent of a 5-foot row grown in an outdoor garden.

Here are some typical container spacings:

How Far Apart to Plant Vegetables in a Container

Vegetable	Space between each plant	Vegetable	Space between each plant
Artichokes	Plant singly	Mustard greens	Thin to 4 inches apart
Beans	3-9 inches apart	Okra	20 inches apart; 5-10 gal. soil per plant
Beets	2-3 inches apart		
Broccoli	10 inches apart; 5 gal. soil per plant	Onions	2-3 inches apart
		Peas	2 inches apart
Brussels sprouts	10 inches apart; 5 gal. soil per plant	Peppers	8 inches apart; 2½ gal. soil per plant
Cabbage	10 inches apart; 5 gal. soil per plant	Potatoes	6 inches apart
Carrots	1-2 inches apart	Radishes	1 inch apart
Cauliflower	12 inches apart; 5 gal. soil per plant	Rhubarb	12 inches apart; 5 gal. soil per plant
		Rutabagas	2 inches apart
Eggplant	15 inches apart; 5 gal. soil per plant	Spinach	Thin to 5 inches apart
		Squash	12-20 inches apart; 5 gal. soil per plant
Kale	Thin to 16 inches apart		
Lettuce	4-10 inches apart	Swiss chard	Thin to 8 inches apart
Melon	15 inches apart; 5 gal. soil per plant	Tomatoes	½-5 gal. soil per plant
		Turnips	6 inches apart

Intercropping and Succession Planting

By intercropping it is quite possible to increase your yields significantly from a single container. This is an extremely valuable technique for an apartment farmer. Intercropping simply means that when you plant vegetables that take a long time to mature, you utilize the in-between space for quick-maturing vegetables. You can, for instance, plant corn on 4- to 5-inch spacing and at the same time plant radishes, green onions, leaf lettuce, turnips, or mustard greens between. Then take the quick-maturing crop out and let the corn grow on to maturity. This multiplies the yield considerably.

You should also keep your crops coming throughout your entire growing season by succession planting. In a 14-inch container planted with carrots, for instance, plant one-third with carrots now, one-third in about two weeks, and one-third two weeks after that. This allows you to harvest a crop over a considerably longer period.

Old-time gardeners have been planting by the moon for years. One gardener I know won't put a thing in the ground if the moon is out of phase. Whether the moon has any influence has not been proved, but some experienced gardeners claim they have great success with this system. It is certainly true that the greatest sum of increasing gravitational forces occurs with the new moon (the lunar gravitation pull that produces high tides in the oceans and water-tides in the soil). If you'd like to experiment with this in your container plantings, here are two general rules as given to me by Grandma Newcomb:

1. *Plant* vegetable seeds two days before the *new* moon and up to seven days afterward.

2. *Transplant* two days before the *full* moon and up to seven days afterward.

If that intrigues you, simply look up the dates of the full moon and new moon in any good almanac, and give it a try. The results may well surprise you.

No-Mess Watering Techniques

Watering your apartment farm need not be a big deal. Pots less than 8 inches in diameter should be watered from above with a 1-quart kitchen measuring cup. Or the entire pot may be half-submerged in a pail of water (or a filled kitchen sink), and when the air bubbles stop coming up from the soil take them out and let them drain. Large containers should be watered from above with a plastic pail or a gentle stream from a hose until the soil is completely saturated.

Don't water again until the soil is dry to a depth of 1 inch. To find out, poke in a finger or take some soil from this depth and rub between the thumb and index finger. If dry, water. If the soil is mud-coated or feels wet, it won't need water for at least twenty-four hours.

Infrequent soakings are much better than overfrequent sprinklings, and after a while you'll have a pretty good idea of how quickly each pot dries out. There are obviously many variables, so you'll have to experiment a bit.

One must not underwater, since vegetables must grow rapidly to maturity and if the soil is allowed to dry out during this time they may develop problems. If the plant is overwatered, the soil becomes waterlogged, forcing air from the soil and suffocating the plant. Some signs for overwatering and underwatering are mentioned when we deal with the specific vegetables.

The worry that your vegetables will dry out during a weekend or a two- or three-day vacation can be avoided in a number of ways.

You can place a few containers in a flat foil pan partially filled with water, or place containers in a bathtub or sink in 2 or 3 inches of water. This method is useful for only a limited time period.

Another good bathtub method is to buy a short section of soaker hose, cut off the last 10 feet and place this over the mouth of the bathtub faucet. Drape the soaker across the containers in the bathtub and turn it on so that it barely drips. This will provide the water they need until you return home. Don't obstruct the drain.

For containers on a windowsill or on the floor, hang a bucket of water above the container (or containers) and run a soft cotton rope from the bottom of the pail to just above the container. Water will be fed down by capillarity and drip into the vegetable container.

For hanging containers (singly or in groups) you can place a pail of water underneath the container and run a piece of soft cotton rope between the water and pot. Water will work its way up the "wick" and into the pot.

You can also give each container a good soaking, then slip a plastic bag over the entire container, sealing it at the bottom with tape. This forms a closed system in which the moisture given off by the plant leaves (transpiration) will return to the soil.

People who get into apartment farming in a big way, planting twenty-five or more containers, often put in a drip system, using a plastic 1-inch pipe and very thin plastic lines that drip water constantly into each container (see illustration).

No-Mess Feeding Techniques

Container vegetables generally need supplemental feedings because the frequent watering leaches out many of the nutrients. Generally, plants need three major elements—nitrogen, phosphorus, and potassium—plus minor and trace elements. Each major nutrient affects vegetable growth different ways. Nitrogen, for instance, is important for the leafy growth of lettuce, mustard, spinach, and other vegetables. Phosphorous is used in flowering and in producing the fruit of eggplant, cucumbers, tomatoes, and peppers. Potassium is necessary for strong root growth and is essential for vigorous growth of carrots, beets, and radishes.

For your apartment farm needs, use either a time-released tomato and vegetable food or a liquid fertilizer.

If you use the time-released tomato and vegetable food, mix it with the "soil" when you originally fill the container at the rate of one tablespoon for each 2 gallons of soil. This will feed your vegetables throughout the growing season.

For liquid fertilizers, make sure it contains 4 to 5 percent phosphorus and use it every two weeks, according to the instructions on the bottle.

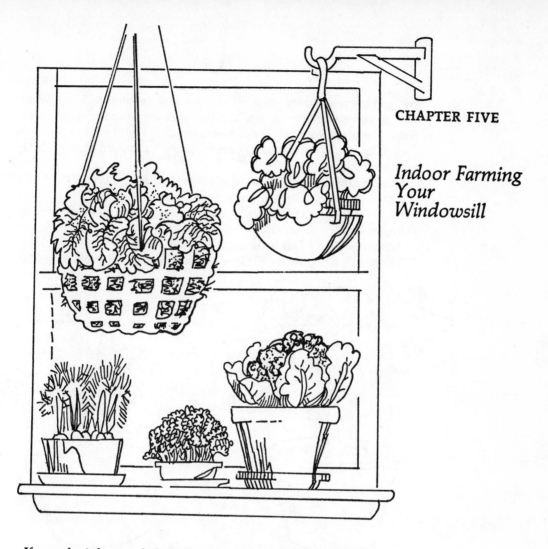

CHAPTER FIVE

Indoor Farming Your Windowsill

If you don't have a balcony, patio, or accessible roof, and you don't want to get into gardening indoors with lights just yet, you can grow plants indoors on windowsills using sunlight.

Suppose you have three rooms with a total of 12 feet of windowsill that receives plenty of sunlight. With this much space you can raise enough salad to feed a family of four for a year. You can farm twenty-five 4-inch pots in which you can grow

—5 or 6 kinds of herbs,

—20 to 30 carrots,

—30 to 35 beets,

—all the radishes you can eat. (Personally, I can only eat one radish a week.)

—enough lettuce for salads all year long,

—even a few tomatoes.

That windowsill space is a potential green mine. Generally,

you can grow anything on a windowsill that requires a 1- or 2-inch spacing between plants, or single plants that keep producing an edible crop. This gives you a choice of five categories:

Sprouts—radish seeds, alfalfa seeds, mung beans, soybeans, wheat, buckwheat, cress.

Salad greens—lettuce, mustard greens, cress, spinach.

Root vegetables—carrots, beets, green onions, garlic.

Herbs—chives, parsley, basil, dill, rosemary, sage, summer savory, tarragon, sweet marjoram.

Tomatoes—Tiny Tim is the most popular.

The details for growing all these are described in Chapters 8 and 10.

Basic Requirements for Gardens on Windowsills

All vegetables have primarily the same requirements. They need enough light to produce good growth, proper temperature, soil with enough nutrients, and the right potting to support good growth and moisture.

Light

The light intensity on any particular windowsill depends on the direction that window faces, whether or not the sun is blocked by a neighboring building, and how much overhang your own building has.

Eastern windows receive two to four hours of gentle morning sun. You generally have enough light in this location to grow radishes, lettuce, and similar vegetables that require only minimal light to reach maturity.

Southern windows receive full sun during most of the day. Here you can grow any vegetable that needs strong light and heat, such as tomatoes or beans.

Western windows receive good light for at least eight hours a day. Generally, you can grow most vegetables in this exposure.

Northern windows receive only diffused light. To grow most vegetables you will need to supplement natural light with artificial light.

Vegetables themselves require different amounts of light, measured in foot-candles, for maximum growth. Tomatoes, for instance, require a minimum of 2,500 foot-candles (bright indirect light) to produce abundantly, radishes require 1,000 foot-candles (about the equivalent of bright shade), and lettuce 1,000 foot-candles. In general, plants require low light intensities—about 1,000 foot-candles—to produce leafy and root growth. Vegetables in which we harvest the fruit—tomatoes, eggplants, squash, and such—need a higher intensity, a minimum of about 2,500 or more foot-candles to reach maturity. However, these vegetables will produce good leafy growth at fairly low light intensities.

Artificial light will do more to pep up your windowsill garden than anything else. If your light is at all minimal here, or if your vegetables do poorly, by all means add a fluorescent fixture, about 6 to 12 inches above the plants with two 40-watt units, one cool-white, one warm-white tube. Simply hang these fixtures from the top of the window on small chains. Start by burning them for two hours a day, and increase that if you are not obtaining good vigorous growth or if your vegetables become spindly. See Chapter 7 for more on artificial light.

One final note here: to make your vegetables grow uniformly on a windowsill, you should turn your plants a little every day or so.

Temperature

It is extremely important to provide the proper growing temperature for your vegetables. As we've seen, vegetables can be roughly divided into cool season and warm season plants. The cool season vegetables (the root and leafy ones) become quite spindly if you keep the room temperature at much over 70 degrees.

It is possible to grow most windowsill vegetables at a room temperature of 60 to 70 degrees.

Most people keep their apartments between 68 and 75 degrees during winter. During summer, the temperature in most apartments stays at about 72 degrees with air conditioning, and 10 to 15 degrees higher than this without it.

If you keep your apartment much over 68 degrees and intend to grow cool season vegetables, consider utilizing a separate room—a back bedroom or a service porch, and just keep the heating ducts closed.

During summer you can grow cool season crops in an air conditioned room. As far as I can see, most vegetables don't mind air conditioning unless you turn the air stream directly on them. Without it, you will either have to switch to warm season vegetables or experiment and see what they'll take and what they won't.

Two cautions: (1) Direct sun (especially in south-facing windows) can bring the temperature a short distance behind the glass to well over 100 degrees. During this time either move your vegetables back or move them to a different exposure. (2) During winter, plants too near cold glass can freeze. Simply move them back far enough to provide an insulation of warm air (4 or 5 inches).

If you have too many plants to move, insulate the plants from the glass by stapling a piece of clear or translucent plastic in front of the window.

Cold drafts coming through cracks around an apartment window can be bad for your vegetables. In addition, drafts dry the soil out more rapidly. When possible, tape the cracks with masking tape or calk with a calking compound.

Soil

Windowsill vegetables are limited by the amount of soil your particular container can hold. The average 4-inch windowsill pot contains 2½ cups of soil. To make sure this quantity of soil will support good vegetable growth, you must adhere rather strictly to spacing requirements. This means two to four carrots, four to eight radishes, and similar quantities of other vegetables in each 4-inch pot. See chart for vegetable quantities in various size pots.

Quantities of Vegetables to Grow in 4-inch and 8-inch Pots

	No. of plants in 4-inch pots	No. of plants in 8-inch pots
Looseleaf lettuce	1	2
Mustard greens	1	3
Spinach	1	2
Beets	2-4	8-20
Carrots	2-4	12-24
Green onions	4-8	16-30
Garlic	2-4	4-16
Turnips	2-4	2-16
Radishes	4-8	16-30

Water

Vegetables must grow rapidly to maturity, which means you must not let the soil dry out. Since 4- to 8-inch pots are susceptible to drying, you should water windowsill pots every morning. Check them every evening. If the soil is dry 1 inch deep (in small pots), add water. You can also prevent excessive drying of containers by setting them in a pan full of moist sphagnum moss.

For ways to keep your plants watered while you're on vacation or away for the weekend, see Chapter 4.

The choice of containers is as wide as your imagination, and although I generally recommend larger pots (8 inches of soil depth) the average windowsill generally limits us to 4-inch pots. This means we need to select our vegetables with care. Here are commonly available items:

Coffee Cans. You can use 1-pound coffee cans quite effectively on a windowsill. Punch drain holes in the sides with a large nail. Place the cans on saucers, or water them in the sink and later put them on the windowsill.

Milk Cartons. Use the half-gallon containers. Cut off 6 to 8 inches above the base and fill with one of the standard mixes. Punch four holes with a pencil around the sides near the base.

Freezer Containers. One-pint freezer containers make great planters. With a pencil punch two or three holes around the sides almost at the base. Plant according to the instructions given in Chapter 4. Water in the sink.

Paper Pots. These are simply pressed paper pots purchased wherever nursery supplies are sold. Treat as a regular 4-inch pot.

Strawberry Plastic Containers. You can easily grow radishes, lettuce, parsley, and similar vegetables in strawberry containers. However, they dry out rapidly, so check frequently and rewater whenever necessary.

There are many things you can do to increase the capacity of your windowsill garden.

1. You can buy an 8-inch-wide board and place it lengthwise on your regular windowsill. It can be held in place with two small nails at either end nailed into the sill and supported by brackets. You can also purchase windowsill extenders from do-it-yourself home centers.

2. You can supplement your space by placing a table directly in front of the windowsill. Also consider utilizing upside-down wicker baskets, old trunks, cable spools, and similar items. They will not only expand your farm but will add a decorative touch to your apartment as well.

3. Place vegetable containers on tables or boxes directly in front of the window. One apartment farmer, for instance, raises corn, zucchini, eggplant, and even peppers in large containers stacked on boxes 6 inches to a foot from the windows.

Windowsill Containers

Increasing the Capacity of Your Windowsill

4. You can hang 8-inch pots either from the top of the window or directly from the ceiling. They not only increase production but add a tremendous aesthetic appeal to your window garden. Support them from the ceiling on an aluminum rod run through the pot and bolted in place with washers. You can purchase the rod and hook from a local variety store. If you are into macrame you can design some extremely attractive hangers that will really set off your apartment. Plant these hanging containers with tomatoes, cucumbers, or similar plants.

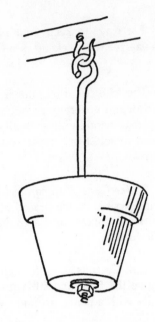

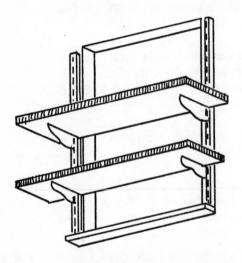

5. To increase capacity even more you can add 8-inch-wide horizontal shelves across the window from top to bottom. They can be held in place with bookcase shelf brackets and standards available at building supply places. Be sure to allow plenty of room between shelves to allow for vegetable growth (this depends on which vegetable you're growing). A 4-foot-high window, for instance, complete with supplemental shelves will allow you to triple production.

6. Add a window greenhouse. Many people who become excited by indoor gardening expand their windowsill gardens by building windowsill greenhouses. A greenhouse, however, even a simple one, is not an activity for a novice to undertake and certainly should not be done without a great deal of planning, since it does involve taking your present window out. Therefore, I suggest you attempt this only when you have the proper tools, materials and plans to work from. Many of the home and garden magazines have advertisements from companies that will provide windowsill garden kits. Take a look at these to see which best fit your home circumstances. *The Handmade Greenhouse:*

From Windowsill to Backyard by Richard Nicholls explains in simple terms just what is involved in creating this exciting extension to apartment farming.

CHAPTER SIX

Outdoor Farming Your Windowbox, Balcony, Patio, or Rooftop

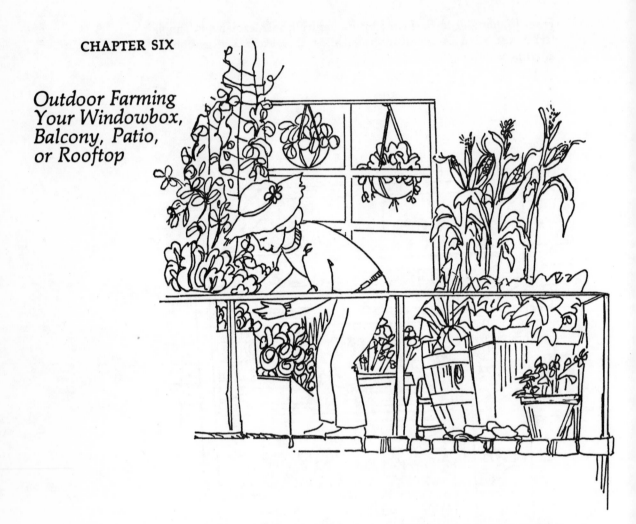

Your balcony or patio offers possibilities you may have never dreamed of. You can grow vegetables in raised box containers. You can have herbs in pots on outdoor wall shelves with beans, cucumbers, and other climbers. You can stack tomatoes, cucumbers, zucchini, and the like in wicker baskets. You can grow beans, cucumbers, and cantaloupes as window and wall curtains, backed up with whiskey-barrel halves of corn, tomatoes, zucchini, and carrots. Your entire garden can be hung 6 feet above the floor from 2-by-4 beams. Building a raised table lets you cultivate all vegetables at table height. You can construct stair-step planters. You may hang your entire garden from the eaves. Or, if you're depressed, you can start up a pot of hemlock.

All vegetables have the same general basic requirements — light, temperature, soil, and water. What varies are the general conditions relative to the area in which they are growing.

If you have six hours of direct sunlight a day on your balcony or patio, you can grow any type of vegetables. Patios, however, have some light problems that the average garden doesn't have. The reflection of direct sunlight on wood, brick, or concrete can produce tremendous heat. Generally, tomatoes, eggplants, and other warm season plants can survive this. But the cool season crops, such as lettuce and radishes, will often be burned. If this is your problem, you will need to protect your plants by hanging bamboo shades, putting up lath protection, stringing 3-inch-wide cloth strips across the patio, or some other method.

Light

A lot depends on individual exposure.

Eastern exposure gets about four hours of gentle morning sun. You can grow leafy and root plants here successfully.

Southern exposure allows you to grow all crops successfully, although you will need to protect lettuce and similar crops. You can cut down on the heat by surrounding your crops with heat-absorbing materials such as peat moss or redwood bark.

Western exposure means you can grow all crops. You generally receive at least six hours of sunlight a day, but you will need to protect your leafy and roof crops from the direct sun.

Northern exposure is extremely limited, although you can probably grow radishes and lettuce. By supplementing your light artificially, however, you can grow other vegetables.

If your patio is partly in the sun, partly in the shade, you can make yourself an aluminum-foil reflector to direct sun into the shady area. One of my apartment neighbors set up two 3-by-9-foot reflectors and now grows a 4-by-8-foot plot of corn, peppers, tomatoes, and eggplant by simply stapling aluminum foil to a piece of plywood and leaning it against the patio wall.

Temperature

Balcony or patio gardening follows outdoor gardening rules, so you have to consult the frost map in Chapter 3 for planting dates. Broccoli, cauliflower, and radishes can be planted two to four weeks before the last killing frost. Beets, cabbage, and carrots can be planted on approximately the last frost. Plant the warm season plants after the days have begun to warm up. Seedlings may be started indoors six to eight weeks before you intend to plant outside. You can also protect plant growth by making jug houses for your plants by cutting off the bottoms of gallon bottles or plastic cleanser jugs and setting the bottomless jugs over the planted seeds. Or you can place a sheet of

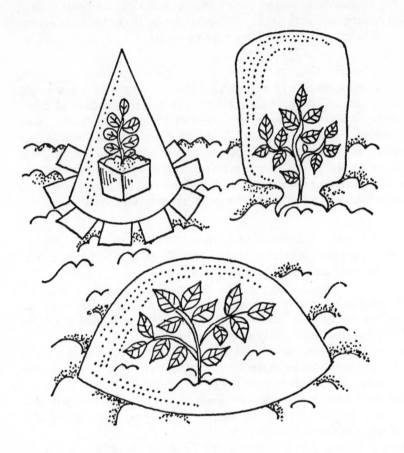

clear plastic across the top of the container (make sure you leave the soil about 4 inches below the top of the container). This provides excellent protection, yet allows you to plant several weeks before the last frost. You can also buy commercially made wax-paper plant protectors called "hot caps" from a nursery. Just make sure that you remove all hot caps, jugs, or plastic sheets on warm days or you'll burn your seedlings.

Soil   Patio containers hold much larger amounts of soil than do indoor containers. Ordinarily this will vary from as little as 2½ cups in small pots to as much as 30 gallons.

Use the All-Purpose Apartment Farmer Soil Mix. In larger containers some apartment farmers like to vary the mix and use garden soil and slow-release fertilizer—one-third rotted manure, one-third garden soil, one-third potting soil—and similar combinations. However, I personally prefer to stay with the standard soil mix.

The requirements are the same for all general containers. Follow the watering rules given in Chapter 4.

The easiest way to start patio vegetable gardening is to simply begin with three or four basic containers and expand as you go along. Here are some of the simplest.

Plastic Pails. Buy yourself some plastic 2- or 3-gallon pails from the local variety store and plant. Or pick up the plastic paint pails (the 5-gallon size) from house building sites where they are thrown away. (Aesthetics is the only drawback. You can, however, cover them with metal foil or place them inside large wicker baskets.) Be sure to punch four or more ¼-inch holes evenly along the sides near the bottom. Put about ½ inch of coarse gravel in the bottom of each container and fill with Apartment Farmer Soil Mix.

Whiskey-Barrel Halves. By law, barrels used once for making whiskey must be discarded, and you can buy barrel halves at many nurseries. Their biggest asset is size, roughly 22 inches across, so they hold enough soil to support good vegetable growth. A single barrel, for instance, will hold seven to eight corn plants, two to three zucchini plants, and two to three tomato plants. You can place them on wheels (purchased at any hardware store) and roll them around the patio. Whiskey barrel gardens are excellent for intercropping. You can intercrop corn with carrots, spinach, radishes, and green onion; tomatoes with radishes, green onions, and lettuce. For other intercropping combinations, simply intersperse crops that require sixty days or more to reach maturity with quick-maturing vegetables (see intercropping chart in Chapter 4).

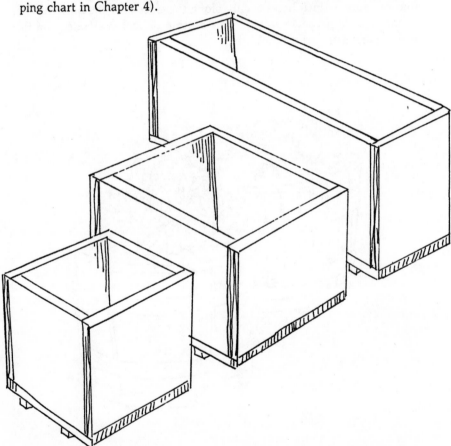

Wooden Boxes. Wooden boxes are excellent for standard patio gardening. Wood has a high insulating value and keeps the hot summer sun of most patio areas from drying the soil out rapidly and damaging the roots. You can buy these boxes from a nursery or make them. Boxes come in many sizes, so consider standard 1-by-1-by-1-foot boxes,

1-by-4-by-1½-foot planter boxes, and 1-by-2-by-2-foot boxes. These will allow you to set varying size boxes under the patio and to utilize them as planters along a wall.

Here's how to make a standard apartment farmer patio container. Materials: Get five 12-by-12-by-1-inch pieces of lumber, 4 feet of 1-by-3-inch boards, cap stock, and 2 feet of 2-by-1-inch stock, a couple dozen 12-penny nails, and a hammer. Nail the pieces together. Add the cap and 2-by-1 cleats at the bottom for feet.

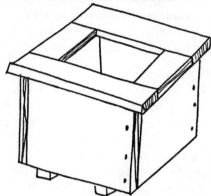

Paper Pulp Pots. Want a container you can lug around without difficulty, can lift easily to fill with soil, and can use as an all-around good vegetable apartment container? Then garden in a paper pulp pot. I recommend using either the 12-inch or 18-inch inside diameter, depending on what you want to plant. For instance, you can plant carrots in the 12-inch pots and eggplant, tomatoes, and other larger plants in 18-inch pots. Water and fertilize according to the instructions in Chapter 4.

Raised Bed Gardening

With standard container patio gardening, you can easily combine containers, furniture, and other patio balcony functions. With raised bed gardens you almost need to turn the entire patio over to gardening. However, the advantages are that the yields are greater in raised beds than they are with any other type of container.

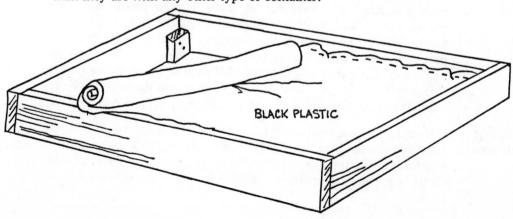

BLACK PLASTIC

Basic raised bed containers consist of four 2-by-8-inch boards nailed together to form a box frame. For the bottom, either line with black plastic on a plywood base. It is best to sketch out your desired farm first on a piece of paper, then build the frames to size. A standard box container is a 1-by-4-foot box made of 1-inch lumber nailed together to make a standard modular container. Fill with Apartment Farmer Soil Mix.

Working height gardens are the last word in raised bed gardens. These are simply box containers supported at table height. Build the tables of 2-by-4s and ½-inch plywood. Make the boxes of ¼-inch plywood and 1-by-10s nailed together. Fill with Apartment Farmer Soil Mix.

Odds and Ends Containers

It isn't necessary, of course, to use formal containers. Actually, part of the fun of apartment farming is using just what's available as vegetable containers. Here are three favorites I'm sure you'll like.

Fruit Box Containers. Fill one with soil, and place it on top of another. Then set five or six around the patio filled with tomatoes, zucchini, corn, or anything else. Just line the box with black plastic (punch holes in the bottom for drainage) and fill with the basic Apartment Farmer Mix. I generally buy these wooden boxes full of apples or pears and save them for my vegetable garden.

Bushel Baskets. These are another attractive container you can scrounge from the back of the supermarket. Again, line with black plastic and fill with soil. They go well with other containers.

Wicker Baskets. These are the most attractive of all. You can use three or four to set off the patio, or several dozen. Buy them at import stores and line with black plastic.

Waterproofing Baskets. You can line them with black plastic, but a more permanent way is to coat the inside of the basket with polyester resin and strips of newspaper to make it waterproof. Buy clear polyester resin and hardener (separately, from a craft store) and a brush. Tear the newspaper into long strips, 5 inches wide. Brush the polyester resin on the basket bottom and sides, then line with the newspaper strips until you have filled the entire inside of the basket. Continue the resin-paper process until you've lined the basket with six coats of paper. When finished, add an additional coat of resin.

Hanging Gardens

Hanging gardens really are the charmers of the apartment farming vegetable world. You can add significantly to your overall patio vegetable production by slipping them in almost anywhere. For instance, you can hang cherry tomatoes 2 feet apart under the eaves, or hang a whole garden of carrots, radishes, and similar plants. Hanging containers will grow all medium-sized vegetables well, including the smaller tomatoes and cucumbers. You generally do not want to plant them with larger vegetables, such as squash, cantaloupe, cabbage, and similar plants.

Here are a few types of hanging containers:

Clay Pots or Containers. You can utilize clay pots quite effectively. Hang standard clay pots with stiff wire, or buy larger clay containers with holes for hanging by ropes.

Wooden Containers. Line wooden baskets with aluminum foil so the soil won't wash through.

Hanging Wire Baskets. Wire baskets make fine containers for lettuce, radishes, even small tomato plants. Stuff the open-wire frame with moist sphagnum moss. You can add burlap if you like. Place an aluminum pie-tin in the bottom to keep soil from washing out. Fill with soil, and pot as you would any other container. A hanging basket dries out very quickly and should be watered daily. To water, simply immerse in a pail of water. You can buy these baskets from most nurseries.

Long, Long Baskets

This is an apartment farmer crop stretcher. Instead of a small wire basket, simply construct a 3- or 4-foot long chicken-wire basket. Cut standard width chicken-wire into 3- and 4-foot lengths, and put the long edges together to form a 3-foot cylinder. Place a small plastic bucket in the end, turn the wire slightly over it, and tie it in place with small pieces of wire. Line the entire container with black plastic. Fill with Apartment Farmer Soil Mix, punch holes in the plastic, and plant vegetables (use peat pots or cubes only). You can, for instance, plant carrots below, then radishes above that, and lettuce at the top.

Vertical Containers

One of the most innovative developments to come along in recent years is vertical vegetable gardening. This makes balcony or patio gardening an entirely different ball game. Now you can plan gardens that go up the walls as high as you can plant and harvest.

The Vegetable Tree. There are a number of variations. For backing, utilize a 2-by-12-inch board any height (generally 6 to 8 feet long). Cut standard chicken wire into 2-foot widths as long as the board. Nail lengthwise to each side of the board. Place a board on the bottom to seal. Line with black plastic, poke holes in the plastic, and fill with Apartment Farmer Soil Mix. You can garden in any combination—for instance, tomatoes at the bottom, cucumbers above, then lettuce, carrots, and radishes at the top. Simply place these along a wall or stand them up at the edge of the patio or balcony. Water and fertilize according to instructions in Chapter 4.

Hanging Basket Trees. The typical hanging basket also comes in a half-round shape for attaching to a flat background. Use a 12-foot-wide board, as above. Attach half-round wire baskets every 2 feet the length of the board. Stuff the frame with moist sphagnum moss. Place an aluminum pie-tin at the bottom to keep the soil from washing out. Fill with Apartment Farmer Soil Mix.

Vegetable Pot Trees. This is simply a vertical variation of pot container gardening. Build a tree with a 4-by-4-inch by 7-foot post, utilizing a Christmas-tree stand base, cross 1-by-3s braced with 1-by-3s. Anchor with bags of sand. Buy pot holders from a hardware store for 8-inch pots and mount alternately up the post. Pot your vegetables in the standard manner. You can place these around the patio, or eliminate the base and nail or mount on a balcony railing.

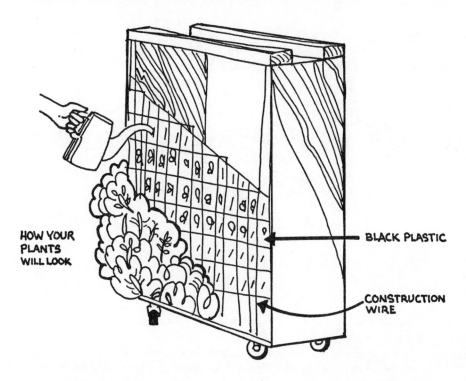

HOW YOUR PLANTS WILL LOOK

BLACK PLASTIC

CONSTRUCTION WIRE

Bookshelf Containers. These are probably the most interesting and most useful of all vertical containers. You can place them throughout the patio area or mount them on wheels and roll around. Bookshelf containers consist of a 2-by-12-inch frame, closed with construction-wire sides, lined with black plastic, and filled with soil mix. A good size is 4 by 5 feet, but make them any size you like. Leave the top open and water from the top, halfway down and two-thirds of the way down. This will thoroughly soak the soil. Before planting, wet the mix, set the transplants through the wire mesh in peat pots, and keep moist. Feed fairly frequently with a liquid plant solution; you can buy this from any garden store.

A-Frame Gardens. While the roll-around bookshelf garden is probably the most versatile, the A-frame garden is the second most. You can set it up in the middle of the patio or in an unused corner. Construct two A-frames with 2-by-4s and a metal sawhorse clamp. A useful one has 5-foot-long, 2-by-4 legs, spread 5 feet apart. Hold the A-units together with a 5-foot 2-by-4. Outside mount three 2-by-8-inch, 6-foot shelves on either side. Use large shelf brackets and brace with 2-by-4s. Place 8-inch pulp-paper pots on the shelves or utilize planter boxes.

Some Rules for Balcony or Patio Gardens

Here are a few basic rules that will help bring order to your balcony or patio farm:

1. Plant the taller vegetables (corn, beans, etc.) either against the walls or on the north side. This will keep the smaller plants from being shaded.

2. For easy harvesting, clump your plants into clusters: (a) tomatoes; (b) lettuce, carrots, radishes, spinach, and similar vegetables; (c) members of the cabbage family, broccoli, cabbage, cauliflower; and (d) other groupings.

3. For root and leafy vegetables (such as radishes) subdivide 12-inch and over containers into two sections: plant half now, half in two weeks.

4. In catch crop containers (in which you plant fast-growing vegetables between slow-growing ones) over 20 inches in diameter, plant corn with radishes, lettuce, green onions, turnips, and other fast-maturing plants.

5. Use vertical and hanging containers whenever possible. This helps multiply your harvest in the same amount of space.

6. Don't limit yourself to vegetables. Plant herbs and flowers such as marigolds or nasturtiums. In containers, of course, you will not get the companion plants effect. But herbs do help repel some insects, and all flowers will add to the beauty of your garden.

Insects

Indoors you have almost no problem, and growing vegetables outdoors on the patio or balcony reduces the insect hazard, but it doesn't eliminate it entirely. One really big advantage to container vegetable gardening, though, is that you can keep your eyes on your plants constantly and start a counterattack almost immediately.

Here are four fairly easy ways to handle insects:

Pick Off the Obvious Insects. The easiest way to get rid of the bigger insects is to watch for them and simply pick them off. This includes beetles, corn earworms, and tomato hornworms. For aphids and scale insects, try soap and water. Mix about 20 tablespoons of soap flakes in 6 gallons of water. You can spray this on with a spray can or pour over the plants from a kitchen measuring cup. This simple solution will eliminate most of your problems.

The Botanical Sprays. There are today some extremely effective botanical sprays that you can buy to eliminate most container vegetable pests: Pyrethrum (made from chrysanthemum flowers), Rotenone (derived from the roots of tropical plants), and Ryania (made from a tropical shrub). You can buy these from your local nursery.

Make Your Own Spray. Old-time gardeners have insisted for years that it's possible to eliminate most insects from the vegetable garden by making up a witches' brew from foul-smelling plants such as garlic, onions, and others. For years we didn't believe them. Then, as the organic gardening movement developed and experimented with organic sprays, we discovered that homemade remedies sometimes work just as well as the more expensive commercial preparations.

Here's a spray that will go a long way toward driving your insects away. Needed ingredients: blender, 1-gallon jug, sprayer, three large onions, one whole garlic, one hot pepper pod. Put the onions, garlic, and pepper in a blender and mix. Cover with water and mix again. Pour into jug and fill to the top with water, shake well. You are now ready to put it in your insect sprayer and go after those bugs with a real vengeance. Also, you need never worry about vampires again.

Chemical Sprays. Chemical pesticides no doubt do the best job of killing most insects, but I would urge you to use the other methods first. However, if the attack becomes particularly bad on your patio vegetables, simply bring out the big guns: Diazinion, Malathion, and Sevin. Diazinion is especially good for controlling root maggots. The other two will handle all other pests.

The best rule is to start easy and move on to other methods only when you really have to. After all, insect attacks run in cycles, and with a little luck those bugs you see in the morning may well move on before you have to do much. If not, break out the artillery and let them have it.

The chart on the following pages gives suggestions on which methods will work best in attacking the pests on your outdoor container vegetables.

Vegetable Diseases

Disease will not be a major container gardening problem, especially since we use a modified "make-up" soil that cuts down the problem. However, it can still happen. A few of the most common diseases you may encounter are mildew (appearing as a white or gray powder or down coating on leaves and stems), rust (appearing first as whitish pustules or warts on the underside of leaves, then as powdery red or brown spores), blight and scab (both appearing as spreading yellow, brown, or red spots on the leaves), and wilt and root rot (both causing decayed roots revealed by the wilting foliage).

There are three ways you can guard against this:

Clean Containers. Dirty pots often harbor disease. To prevent this, scrub your containers before repotting each season. For small pots, simply fill the sink with soapy water and scrub with a small vegetable brush. For larger containers, empty the container into a garbage can, then scrub with a brush and a pan full of soapy water. Rinse with boiling water. After that, refill and plant.

Disease-Resistant Varieties. Currently there are many vegetable varieties resistant to the major diseases. You can buy, for instance, cabbage strains resistant to virus yellows; cucumber strains resistant to anthracnose, down mildew, mosaic, powdery mildew, and scab; snap beans resistant to mosaic, powdery mildew, and root rot. You can buy these and other disease-resistant varieties from seed racks or seed catalogs. The catalog description or seed package labels will state the diseases to which the varieties are resistant.

Chemical Fungicides. You will probably not need to utilize these, but if your plants are hit by disease, both Captan and Phaltan are quite effective for control. Mildew may sometimes appear on your vegetable leaves as a white gray powder because of overwatering or poor air circulation. To correct, move to different location, water less, or spray with sulfur dust.

What Kind of Control Do You Use for What Pest?

Vegetable	Symptoms	Pests
Artichokes	Colonies of insects on leaves and buds	Snails and Slugs
Beans	Colonies of black sucking insects on leaves	Aphids
	Circular holes eaten in leaves	Bean leaf beetles
	Small plants cut off at soil level at night	Cutworm
	Hopping, running insects that suck sap from leaves	Leafhoppers
	Lower surface of leaves eaten between veins; skeletonized	Mexican bean beetles
	Scaly nymphs on underside of leaves; white adults flutter about when disturbed	Whiteflies
Beets	Leaves eaten, leaving trail of silver slime	Snails and slugs
Broccoli	Colonies of small green insects on leaves	Aphids
	Plants sickly; maggots attack underground parts of plant	Cabbage maggots
	Holes in leaves eaten by larvae	Cabbage worms and loopers
	Small plants cut off at soil level at night	Cutworms
Brussels Sprouts	Colonies of small insects on leaves	Aphids
	Plants sickly; maggots attack underground parts of plant	Cabbage maggots
	Holes eaten in leaves by larvae	Cabbage worms and loopers
	Small plants cut off at soil level at night	Cutworms
Cabbage	Colonies of small insects on leaves	Aphids
	Plants sickly; maggots attack underground parts of plant	Cabbage maggots
	Holes eaten in leaves by larvae	Cabbage worms and loopers
	Small plants cut off at soil level at night	Cutworms

Pick off	Spray with soap solution	Spray with Pyrethrum	Spray with Rotenone	Spray with Ryania	Put out containers of beer	Use Sevin	Use Malathion	Use Diazinion
	X	X	X	X	X		X	
	X	X	X	X			X	
X		X	X	X		X		
						X		X
		X	X	X		X	X	
X		X	X	X			X	
		X	X			X	X	X
					X			
	X	X	X	X			X	
								X
X		X				X		
						X		X
	X	X	X	X			X	
								X
X		X				X		
						X		X
	X	X	X	X			X	
								X
X		X				X		
						X		X

What Kind of Control Do You Use for What Pest?

Vegetable	Symptoms	Pests
Cauliflower	Colonies of small green insects on leaves	Aphids
	Plants sickly; maggots attack stems and underground parts of plant	Cabbage maggots
	Holes in leaves eaten by larvae	Cabbage worms and loopers
Corn	Silks cut off at ear; kernels destroyed by fairly large larvae	Corn earworms
	Ears and stalks tunneled by larvae	Corn borers
	Small plants cut off at soil level at night	Cutworms
Cucumber	Colonies of small insects on underside of leaves	Aphids
	All parts eaten	Cucumber beetles
	All parts of vines eaten	Pickleworm
Eggplant	Plant defoliated (beetlew are black striped, larvae brick red)	Colorado potato beetles
	Colonies of small insects on underside of leaves	Aphids
	Colonies on underside of leaves	Eggplant lacebugs
Lettuce	Colonies of small insects on leaves	Aphids
	Leaves eaten by pincer bugs	Earwigs
	Wedge-shaped insects found on leaves; tips of leaves turn brown	Leafhoppers
	Leaves eaten, leaving trails of silver slime	Snails and slugs
Kale	Colonies of small insects on leaves	Aphids
	Small pin-size holes chewed in leaves	Flea beetles
Melons	Colonies of small insects on underside of leaves	Aphids
	All parts of plant eaten	Cucumber beetles
Mustard Greens	Colonies of small insects on leaves	Aphids
	Leaves with holes eaten by larvae	Cabbage worms
	Plants sickly; maggots attack root and stem underground	Root maggots
Onions	Older leaves wither; small yellow insects feed at base of leaves	Onion thrips
	Plants sickly; maggots attack parts below ground	Onion maggots

Pick off	Spray with soap solution	Spray with Pyrethrum	Spray with Rotenone	Spray with Ryania	Put out containers of beer	Use Sevin	Use Malathion	Use Diazinion
	X	X	X	X			X	
								X
X			X			X		
X				X		X		
X						X		
						X		X
	X	X	X	X			X	
X		X	X	X		X		X
X		X	X			X	X	X
X		X	X	X		X		X
	X	X	X	X			X	
		X	X				X	
			X				X	
	X	X	X	X			X	
		X	X	X		X	X	
					X			
	X	X	X	X			X	
X		X	X	X		X		X
	X	X	X	X			X	
X		X	X	X		X		X
	X	X	X	X			X	
X			X			X		
								X
		X	X	X			X	
								X

What Kind of Control Do You Use for What Pest?

Vegetable	Symptoms	Pests
Okra	Holes eaten in pods	Corn earworms
Peas	Terminals deformed; colonies of small insects on leaves	Pea aphids
	Beetles feed on blooms; larvae bore through pod and enter young peas	Pea weevils
Peppers	Colonies of small insects on leaves	Aphids
	Plants defoliated by orange and yellow-bodied beetles	Blister beetles
	Small plants cut off at soil level at night	Cutworms
	Small pin-size holes chewed in leaves	Flea beetles
	Leaves and fruit eaten	Pepper weevils
Radishes	Plants sickly; maggots attack plants below ground	Root maggots
Spinach	Colonies of small insects on leaves	Aphids
	Larvae tunnel through leaves	Spinach leaf miners
Squash	Colonies of small insects underneath the leaves	Aphids
	All parts eaten	Cucumber beetles
	Plants wilted (brownish flat bug)	Squash bug
	Sudden wilting of runners; holes in stem near base	Squash vine borer
Swiss Chard	Colonies of small insects on leaves	Aphids
Tomatoes	Colonies of small insects on leaves	Aphids
	Small plants cut off at soil level	Cutworms
	Many shot-size holes in leaves	Flea beetles
	Leaves eaten (large green worm with horn)	Tomato hornworm
	Scale-like nymphs attached to underside of leaves	Whiteflies

Pick off	Spray with soap solution	Spray with Pyrethrum	Spray with Rotenone	Spray with Ryania	Put out containers of beer	Use Sevin	Use Malathion	Use Diazinion
X				X		X		
	X	X	X	X			X	
X								
	X	X	X	X			X	
X		X	X	X				
						X		X
X		X	X	X		X		X
								X
	X	X	X	X			X	
			X					
	X	X	X	X			X	
X		X	X	X		X		X
X		X	X	X		X		
						X		
	X	X	X	X			X	
	X	X	X	X			X	
						X		X
		X	X	X		X		X
X		X	X					
		X	X				X	

CHAPTER SEVEN

*Indoor Farming
Your Bedroom
(or Closet, Attic,
or Basement) with
Artificial Lights*

It's a great feeling to be able to serve a salad in February that you've just picked a few minutes ago from your own indoor farm. There are a lot of vegetables you can grow indoors under lights all winter long.

Some vegetables are easy to grow (mostly the root and leafy vegetables), some are possible to grow (like tomatoes), and others are better grown as seedlings under lights, then transplanted into containers for windowsill or balcony gardens. You can grow spinach, radishes, carrots, beets, lettuce, some herbs, Chinese cabbage, celery, endive, green onions, cucumbers, parsley, watercress, tomatoes. For transplant, you can grow cabbage, broccoli, Brussels sprouts, cauliflower, zucchini, beans, peppers, cantaloupes, and eggplants. This means, then, that you can grow all root and leafy vegetables to maturity under lights, and start the ones that produce an edible fruit (like a zucchini or a bean, for instance). Generally, however, these take too much light intensity to bring to maturity in our apartment farm.

Your indoor-light gardens are limited only by your imagination, since you're providing your own light. Consider empty kitchen cabinets, closets with additional shelves, inside bookshelves. You generally don't have to worry about mold, but it's better not to keep clothes in the same closet as plants.

If you want to start growing vegetables indoors the quick, easy, utilitarian way, just set up your plants in a corner of the room on an old 3-by-4-foot table, buy a standard 4-foot reflector fixture that will hold two to four fluorescent tubes, and mount the fixture 6 to 18 inches above the table surface—two to four 40-watt fluorescent tubes (warm- to cool-white) for every 4 feet of table space you want to illuminate.

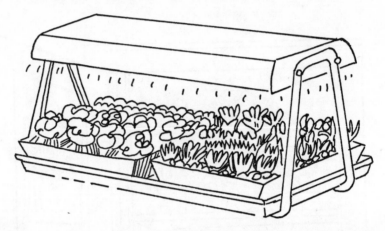

There are also a number of commercial units you can simply go out and buy at a garden center. These vary from a simple two-bulb unit with a stand and tray to two four- and eight-tray stands up to 6 feet high.

Let's look now at light, temperature, soil, nutrients, and water and see exactly what's required to successfully grow vegetables under artificial light.

If you have the basic setup, however, don't be overly concerned about getting just the right number of foot-candles for each vegetable. As you go along and learn what the maximum conditions are in your apartment, you can make the adjustments for greater light when necessary. There is a book, *Gardening Indoors Under Lights*, which goes into details on this subject for the dedicated indoor vegetable grower. For those who are simply having the fun of growing some vegetables inside year round, the exact foot-candle measurements are not all that necessary.

How to measure foot-candles: If you have a camera with a built-in light meter, that only gives you an exposure setting, set the film speed at ASA 100 and aim the meter at a white piece of paper placed so as to approximate the plant leaf surface position. The shutter speed reading that will appear opposite f4 will correspond to the approximate foot-candles of illumination. For example, if the indicated exposure is 1/250 second at f4, this will be 250 foot-candles.

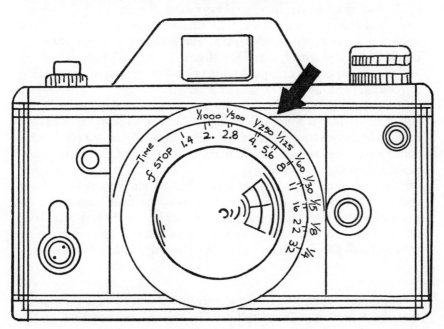

Cool-white tubes have a lot of blue light (and a lot of intensity) and are good for vegetative growth. The warm-white has more of the red spectrum. For growing leafy vegetables you can simply use two cool white tubes instead of the combination cool-white and warm-white.

As with watering and temperature, it's wonderful if you can obtain the ideal light conditions for the growth of your vegetables. But just as there are cloudy summers and rainy summers, and hot and cold summers which vary quality of vegetables grown in the ground, so there will be variations in your apartment. The standard apartment fixture contains two 40-watt fluorescent lamps with a 12-inch reflector and is adequate for many vegetables. It provides approximately 860 foot-candles, if the plants are 6 inches beneath the tubes. Generally, leafy and root vegetables need about 1,000 foot-candles for proper growth. To solve that problem, you can utilize a unit that will hold four fluorescent lamps. To know exactly how many foot-candles of illumination you have, check with the easy camera light meter method shown in the diagram.

Light

Vegetables need both the visible and the invisible light rays for healthy, vigorous growth. In actuality, the vital rays are the blue (450 nanometer units), the red (650 nanometer units), and the far-red (730 nanometer units). A nanometer is the scientific unit for measuring light waves—and now that we know that, we'll never mention it again in this book. Sunlight provides these vital rays naturally. But both fluorescent tubes and the common electric light (the incandescent bulb) produce only a portion of the needed rays. Fluorescent tubes, for instance, produce blue and red rays, and the electric light bulb produces the red and far-red rays. You can grow most vegetables, however, by utilizing fluorescent light, as we'll explain in a minute.

Surprisingly enough, when you start growing vegetables under lights, you discover that it's just not enough to turn on the lights. I have a friend who, when he discovered gardening under lights, simply put his plants under the bulbs and left them there. At first the plants grew rapidly, then the stems began to shrivel and the leaves looked bad. His problem was that plants need darkness. Not so much to produce leafy and root growth, but to blossom and produce fruit. Generally, all vegetables need fourteen to eighteen hours of light and short periods of darkness. If you keep the fluorescent tubes burning constantly, your tomatoes will go wild (foliage-wise) but just won't produce tomatoes.

What Lights to Buy

Fluorescent Tubes. You cannot simply go out and buy any fluorescent tube and expect to get good results. The time-proven combination for growing plants indoors is the *cool-white* together with a *warm-white* tube. *Do not buy* lamps with the designation (it's printed in small letters on the end of the tube) *white* or *daylight*. These are not adapted for plant growth. A fluorescent tube will generally last about two years, but should really be changed after about a year since the efficiency falls off.

A fluorescent fixture with two, three, or four 4-feet-long 40-watt tubes in a reflector will light a growing area of 2 to 4 feet. Two fixtures mounted parallel will illuminate a 3-by-4-foot area. Two 8-foot, two-tube industrial fixtures (side by side) will light a 3-by-8-foot area (placed 12 to 15 inches above the plants).

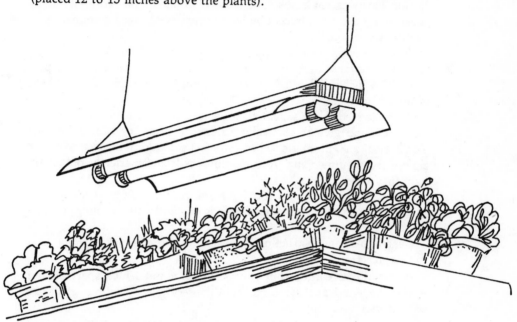

Special Plant-Growth Lamps (Grow-Lights). These are fluorescent phosphor lamps developed especially to use in the home for plant growth and sold commercially as Gro-Lux, Plant-Light, and Plant Gro tubes. These lamps reduce the output of the yellow-green rays of the spectrum (which are not useful for plant growth) and increase the production of red and blue rays (which are). Some gardeners swear by them; others say you will do just as well using a standard warm-white and cool-white tube together.

Fixtures. Fixtures come in many sizes and lengths for special gardening conditions (in a closet or bookshelf, for instance). For these areas, simply buy the narrow boxlike channel fixtures (without reflectors). Then you can mount them close together to adapt to your own needs. They come in almost any length, and you can get them at any home supply or electrical store. The best way is to suspend the light fixture on chains or pulley ropes.

However, if you intend to really turn out quantities of vegetables, the best unit you can have is a basic A-frame, 5 feet long by 3 feet wide, with three shelves. These hold tremendous quantities of vegetables in little space. You can build one out of 2-by-4 lumber. You will need fluorescent units for each shelf.

Growing Seedlings Under Lights

One of the best ways to use lights is to grow seedlings for later transplanting into your containers. Generally, you can grow seedlings with two 40-watt cool white fluorescent bulbs. Some apartment farmers, however, prefer the fluorescent fixtures in combination with two 25-watt incandescent bulbs. The reason is that the far-red light energy provided by the incandescent bulbs is necessary for seed germination of light-sensitive seeds.

Fluorescent lamps can provide both heat for sprouting seeds and light to grow seedlings. In sprouting seeds, position your seed pans or peat pots 3 or 4 inches below the tubes, then burn them constantly until the seedlings emerge.

Once the seeds have sprouted, place the seedlings 6 to 9 inches from the tubes, and give them twelve to sixteen hours of sunlight a day. You'll find an automatic timer an excellent addition since you can simply set the timer and your seedlings will automatically obtain the light they need.

Don't move your tubes too far from your seedlings, because at a greater distance, the light intensity falls off, and your seedlings become spindly.

General planting instructions for seedlings is gone into in some detail in Chapter 4.

As mentioned earlier, thin your seedlings about 1 inch apart as soon as the true leaves appear. (Simply cut the seedlings off with a small pair of scissors.)

Temperature

Cool season vegetables like temperatures below 65 degrees. Warm season vegetables grow and mature best in temperatures above 65 degrees (to about 90). It is difficult to satisfy both these needs indoors, yet it's possible to achieve a reasonable balance somewhere between 60 and 70 degrees. Actually, night temperatures are the important ones in vegetable production, and leafy and root vegetable production is greatly enhanced if you can bring the temperatures for these vegetables down between 50 and 60 degrees at night; 60 to 70 is okay for the others.

Soil, Nutrients, Water

These are about the same as for other container plants. Follow the instructions given in Chapter 4.

CHAPTER EIGHT

Basic Vegetables for Your Apartment Farm

Generally, you can grow any vegetables in your apartment farm that you can grow in a regular garden—even winter squash, if you've got the space. There are only a few vegetables, like asparagus, that aren't really suited for containers. But despite the fact that you garden in a limited space, you have a decided advantage over an out-in-the ground gardener since you can reach your entire crop in four or five steps. There aren't many farmers who would try to survey the south forty in their slippers.

Apartment farmers indulge their whims far more than any other kind of farmers do. I know one indoor gardener who loved corn so much that he grew nothing but corn on a 10-by-15-foot sunny patio. Viewed from a certain angle, it looked exactly like a midwestern corn field. When I mentioned that his was some of the finest corn I'd ever seen, he said, "The first year it didn't do so well, so the next year I put up a big sign in the patio that said KANSAS, and now it just gets better every season." (I've always believed in talking to my plants, but I never thought they could read before.)

That's the way of apartment farming. It just keeps getting better and better.

In this chapter, I will describe, in alphabetical order, the vegetables that grow in containers, and tell you how easy or difficult they are to manage. Mini-vegetables, novelties, and gourmet vegetables are described in following chapters. When considering individual vegetables you should begin to think ahead to picking time. The trick is to catch them when the sugar (or flavor) content is highest.

The general rule is to try to pick vegetables before they are completely mature, then cook them as soon as possible. Vegetables picked this way are far tastier than anything you can buy in the supermarket, because by the time store vegetables travel from the commercial grower to the wholesale market to the store they've lost a great deal of their flavor. In addition, of course, commercial varieties are not usually the tastiest anyway, since they are generally grown for commercial qualities, such as size, color, and durability on supermarket shelves.

Spring and Fall Cool Weather Crops for Patios

Broccoli
Kale
Lettuce
Spinach
Turnips
Peas

Greatest Yield Vegetable for Apartment Farm Space

Tomatoes	30-100 cherry tomatoes per 8-inch pot
Bush snap beans	10-20 bunches per 12-inch pot
Lettuce	Enough in an 8-inch pot for 10-30 salads if leaves picked when needed
Zucchini	10-40 per 5-gal. container
Carrots	16-60 per 8-inch pot
Beets	16-20 per 8-inch pot
Radishes	30-40 per 8-inch pot
Onions	30 green onions per 8-inch pot

Vegetables that Mature Quickly

Radishes	22 days
Mustard greens	35 days
Loose-leaf lettuce	40 days
Green onions	40 days
Spinach	42 days
Turnips	45 days
Bush snap beans	45 days
Summer squash	50 days
Early peas	55 days
Kale	55 days

Light Most leafy and root vegetables can be grown with two 40-watt fluorescent tubes, if the tubes are suspended 3 to 6 inches above the plant, to produce approximately 1,000 foot-candles of light. Check this with the camera lightmeter technique on p. 69.

Utilize the All-Purpose Apartment Farmer Soil Mix. Here it is again: **Soil**

1/2 gallon each of:
Commercial potting mix
Compost (purchased or homemade)
Common garden soil

Water pots less than 8 inches in diameter from above with a kitchen **Water** measuring cup. Or half submerge the pots in a sink full of water, and take them out when the soil stops bubbling.

Water large containers with a plastic pail or with a gentle stream from a hose until the soil is completely saturated.

When the soil is dry to a depth of 2 inches, water again. To find out, poke in a finger or take some soil from this depth and rub between the thumb and index finger. If dry, water. If the soil is mud-coated or feels wet, the plant won't need any more water for twelve to twenty-four hours.

Use a tomato-vegetable time-released fertilizer mixed into the soil **Supplemental** when you plant your vegetables at the rate of 1 tablespoon per 2 gallons **Fertilization** of soil. This should be sufficient throughout the life of most vegetables. Or utilize a commercial liquid fertilizer that contains at least 4 to 5 percent phosphorus. Feed every two weeks according to instructions.

Cool season plant. Rated fair for outdoor containers.

A large, decorative, silver-green plant that really sets off a patio, this thistlelike perennial vegetable can spread as much as 6 feet. The flower buds ripen into large, pink thistle blossoms that can be used around your apartment in dried arrangements.

How to Grow. Artichokes need at least 10 gallons of container soil. You can purchase artichoke roots for planting from a local nursery or

Artichoke

send for them from seed catalogs. To plant, dig a small hole in the middle of the container for the artichoke root, position the root vertically, and cover with soil, keeping the base of the leafy shoots just above the soil line. Plant root divisions (buy these from your local nursery) in patio containers during early spring. If you're starting from seed, plant six to seven weeks earlier in peat pots and transplant directly into the container. Where winters are cold, cut back the tops in the fall to 12 inches. Tie the old stalks over the root crown, cover with torn newspapers.

Varieties to Grow

Green Globe

How to Use. The plant is large, so utilize singly as a decorative plant on the patio. It can be grown indoors behind a window if the plant is shaded during the summer (the main problem, of course, is space).

Under Lights. Artichokes will grow with two 40-watt fluorescent units. Because of size, they must be transplanted into patio containers.

Typical Problems. None—at least not enough to worry about.

Harvesting Tips. Cut the buds before they begin to open. Leave a 1½-inch length of stem on each bud after cutting. When the major stem has dried out after fruiting, remove it with a kitchen knife. New fruiting shoots will form during the season. Now, if there were only a way to grow a tub of melted butter.

Asparagus   This is not a good container plant because of the wide-spreading root system.

Beans   *Warm season crop. Rated good for outdoor containers, poor for indoor containers.*
Beans, beans everywhere—the problem is which ones to plant. Container gardeners go crazy with beans. First you have to choose between bush beans, which grow 15 to 20 inches tall, and snap beans (the climbing types), which grow up poles 5 to 8 feet high. Then, as if that weren't enough, you can plant lima beans, soybeans, fava beans, and southern cowpeas—which is certainly enough to leave anybody's bean in a whirl. Many apartment farmers like to grow bush beans because they can grow three to six plants in a large container. Others like to experiment with all the bean types.

76

How to Grow. Allow at least 8 to 12 inches of container soil for all beans. (Except jellybeans—they do better in a clean, dry box.)

Bush Beans. Plant 3 inches apart in containers. Plant pole (snap) beans 9 to 12 inches apart. Cover both with 1½ inches of soil. Water.

Lima Beans. These come in both bush and pole types and are planted much like snap beans except they need more space. Plant 4 to 6 inches apart, 2 inches deep. Plant on edge to improve chances of germination.

Soybeans. These do well in warm, humid climates. Grow as you would lima beans.

Fava Beans. These grow 3 to 4½ feet high and have long, rather flattened green pods and meaty seeds. Fava beans require long periods of cool weather to mature. Plant in early spring (summer or late fall in mild winter climates). Plant 3 to 4 inches apart, and cover with 2 inches of soil.

Cowpeas. Many gardeners think of these as peas; however, they resemble beans in appearance and garden needs. Cowpeas need about four months of warm weather to mature. Plant 3 to 4 inches apart, and cover with 1 inch of container soil.

Outdoor Planting. Plant bush and snap beans as soon as the soil temperature reaches 65 degrees and above (check by pushing kitchen thermometer in the soil).

Varieties to Grow

	Days to Maturity	
Bush green		
Tendercrop	53	Dark green, slender pods
Topcrop	49	Medium green, hardy
Greensleeves	56	Dark-green pods, white-seeded
Bush wax		
Burpee's Brittle Wax	52	Lemon-yellow pods, hardy
Bush purple		
Royalty Purple Pod	51	Purple pods that cook green

Pole snap		
Kentucky Wonder	65	Large green pods, heavy producer
Burpee Golden	60	Flat pods, butter yellow, tender
Bush lima		
Burpee's Improved Bush Lima	75	Grows in clusters of 5-6 pods
Fordhook 242	75	Big-seeded
Pole lima		
Prizetaker	90	Extremely large beans
King of the Garden	88	Old favorite, pods about 5 inches long
Bush soybean		
Kanrich	103	Erect bushlike plants
Fava beans (bush)		
Long Pod	85	Pods glossy green, 7 inches long
Bush shell beans		
Red Kidney	95	Large, kidney-shaped, pinkish red
Cowpeas		
California Blackeye	75	Pods 7-8 inches long

How to Use. Plant either in containers or boxes, and run on strings over a window or up a wall. Insert a 2-by-2-inch post in a whiskey-barrel half, and grow beans up strings. Attach a garden trellis to the back of a large container, and grow beans up strings.

Under Lights. Beans are difficult to grow under lights. Plant in patio containers or in window boxes. Bean seedlings for transplants can be started in peat pots with two 40-watt fluorescent tubes.

Typical Problems. *My beans just don't come up.*
You planted outdoors in containers too early. Plant in peat pots indoors and transfer to your patio containers after the soil warms up.
My vines look good, but I never get much of a crop. You aren't picking the overmature pods. Leaving a few old pods on the vines will greatly reduce the oncoming crop.
Part of my bean pods shrivel at the end. you have let the soil dry out. Keep the soil moist, according to the instructions in Chapter 4.

Harvesting Tips. Pick pods when the sides are just starting to bulge and before they start to become tough and stringy. The more frequently you pick your beans, of course, the more the vines will produce.

Cool season crop. Rated excellent for outdoor and indoor containers.   **Beets**
Beets are tremendous container plants for the apartment farmer, since you can grow a large quantity in a small space. In addition, beet leaves are extremely decorative, and you can harvest these leaves for greens and eat the bulbous root as well.

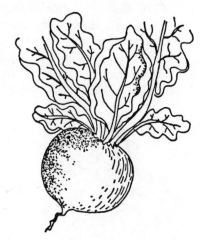

How to Grow. Scatter the beet seeds on a 2-inch spacing over the entire container surface. Cover with ¼ inch of mix and keep moist. Thin later to about 3 inches apart. Plant large containers in at least two sections, half of the total space now, half in two to three weeks.

Inside, plant any time. Outside, in patio containers, start planting beets on the approximate date of the last frost. (See frost map, Chapter 3.) Plant in October and November for a crop in December, January, and February.

Varieties to Grow

	Days to Maturity	
Detroit Dark Red	60	Round with deep-red skin
Early Wonder	55	Semiglobe
Cylindra	60	A long cylindrical beet

4-Inch Pot Tips. Grow two to three beets per 4-inch pot.

Under Lights. You can grow beets successfully with two 40-watt fluorescent tubes.

Typical Problems. *My beets just didn't come up.* Beets are a little slow to sprout. In addition, they germinate poorly if they aren't kept moist throughout the entire germination period. Plant again.

My container beets didn't get very big. You just couldn't bear to thin your beets. Make sure there is at least a 1-inch spacing between young plants, 2 to 3 inches later.

Harvesting Tips. Begin pulling beets to eat as soon as they reach ¼ inch in diameter. This will allow the remaining beets to become considerably larger. Do not let beets become giant-size, as they may become woody.

Broccoli   *Cool season crop. Rated fair for outdoor containers.*

Here's a vegetable that can really put a strain on a container. It grows 3 or 4 feet high and branches prolifically. Once you get your broccoli started producing, it just keeps on and on for weeks. In recent years, fortunately, breeders have tremendously increased the size of the central head while at the same time reducing the overall plant size.

How to Grow. You can grow broccoli in 5- to 10-gallon containers. Buy small plants from your local nursery or grow your own in peat pots and transfer to a container. Plant only one broccoli plant to a container.

Plant in the spring, a couple of weeks before the last frost (see frost map, Chapter 3), so the plants will mature before the days become really hot. In many areas you can then plant again in midsummer for a fall crop. If you prefer starting from seeds, plant in peat pots ¼ inch deep about five to six weeks before you intend to plant in containers.

Varieties to Grow

	Days to Maturity	
Green Comet Hybrid	40	Single heads 6-7 inches across
De Cicco-Burpee's Greenbud Brand	60	High production of side sprouts, silver
Premium Crop Hybrid	58	All-American medal winner, central head 8-9 inches across

How to Use. Plant outside in single containers on the patio.

Under Lights. Broccoli can grow 1 foot tall in eight weeks under lights and keep right on going if you'll give it the space. You can't very well grow it to maturity this way, however. Grow 6- to 7-inch-high seedlings under two 40-watt fluorescent tubes, then transfer to outdoor containers.

Typical Problems. *My broccoli suddenly goes to flower.* It's getting too much heat. Shade the plants with cheesecloth, or bring inside into a cool area when the weather turns warm.

Harvesting Tips. Cut the terminal bud 5 inches below the head on the edible stem. The plant will soon send up additional shoots. To encourage production, keep the shoots harvested.

Cool season crop. Rated excellent for indoor, fair for outdoor containers.

Brussels Sprouts

This is the apartment farmer's one-man, or woman, food machine. Once it starts producing (sprouts that look like tiny cabbages), you think it's going to keep on turning them out forever. These members of the cabbage family grow extremely large in containers, with the sprouts clustered tightly around the tall, main stem.

How to Grow. Plant one plant per 5- or 10-gallon container from seedlings (either purchase from a local nursery or grow your own from seeds planted ½ inch deep in peat pots). As the plants mature, remove all excess leaves, except those at the top. Brussels sprouts require four to five months of cool weather to mature. They do well during the summer if you live in an area where the climate is moist and averages 65 degrees or less. If you live in a warmer area, set the plants out on your patio in early summer so they will mature in the cooler fall weather.

Varieties to Grow

	Days to Maturity	
Jade Cross Hybrid	80	Blue-green sprouts, 22-inch plants
Long Island Improved	90	Dark-green heads

How to Use. Plant in single containers on the patio as a conversation piece. You can also grow a single plant in front of a window during the winter (supplement a north-facing window with one hour of fluorescent light each day (two 40-watt tubes). Brussels sprouts do best at a temperature between 60 and 65 degrees.

Under Lights. Brussels sprouts grow extremely well under two 40-watt fluorescent tubes, but can't be grown to maturity because of their size. Transfer to a container for growth outdoors or indoors in front of a window.

Typical Problems. Practically none, except the temperature problem.

Harvesting Tips. Snap or trim off the sprouts when they are firm and deep green. They taste best when the sprouts are about 1 to 1½ inches in diameter. Mild frost simply improves the flavor. Pick the lowest sprout each time, and break off any leaves left below the sprout. Don't remove the top leaves.

Cabbage

Cool season crop. Rated fair for outdoor containers, poor for indoor containers.

Cabbage is a natural performer for the apartment farmer, since it comes in many different colors and loves to show off. Especially good for container show-offs are the Reds and the Savoy cabbage.

How to Grow. Most apartment farmers buy seedlings from a nursery rather than start from seed. Plant two cabbage plants per 3- to 5-gallon container, then thin out the weakest in a few weeks. Cabbage is a heavy feeder, so give double Apartment Farmer feedings twice a week. Make sure that the soil does not dry out, since cabbage is especially susceptible to a lack of water.

If you want to start cabbage from seed, sow the seeds ½ inch deep in aluminum pans or peat pots about six to eight weeks before you intend to transplant the plants indoors. For outside containers, plant cabbage to mature during cool weather. Plant either before or after the hot weather. Plant seedlings early spring or late summer.

Make sure you do not repot cabbage in containers which have already grown cabbage plants. I ordinarily make it a practice to get rid of the soil I have grown cabbage in and replace with new soil. This precaution is necessary to reduce the risk of common cabbage diseases.

Varieties to Grow

	Days to Maturity	
Early		
Early Jersey Wakefield	63	Conical heads, 2-3 pounds
Copenhagen Market	72	Medium, 4-4½ pounds
Late		
Danish Ball-head	105	Weighs more for size than any other cabbage
Red (these are great for decorating)		
Mammoth Red Rock	100	Tight, deep purplish; red heads
Red Acre	76	Deep red, medium-sized
Ruby Ball Hybrid	68	All-American winner, dark-red color
Savoy (extremely decorative)		
Savoy King Hybrid	90	Crinkled green leaves
Perfection Drumhead	90	Large heads
Chieftain Hybrid	90	Firm heads

How to Use. Cabbage should be grown individually in large containers as a show-off. Give it space by itself. You can also move it inside on special occasions as a conversation piece, or grow one plant in front of a window all year long.

Under Lights. Cabbage will grow with good vigor under two 40-watt fluorescent tubes for transplanting. (Keep the temperature between 60 and 65 degrees.)

Typical Problems. *My cabbage heads split, especially the early varieties.* Any time you slow down the water supply and then resume it again, cabbage heads will crack. You should make sure your container soil doesn't dry out. Also, you can halt cracking by holding off on water when the cracking begins, or twist the plant to break off some of the roots; these actions slow the growth process.

Harvesting Tips. Begin harvesting heads when they are firm and still fairly small. Leave a few leaves near the main head to support lateral growth.

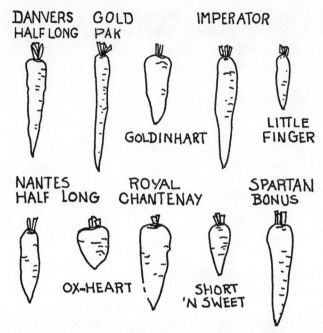

DANVERS HALF LONG   GOLD PAK   IMPERATOR

GOLDINHART

LITTLE FINGER

NANTES HALF LONG   ROYAL CHANTENAY   SPARTAN BONUS

OX-HEART

SHORT 'N SWEET

Carrots   *Cool season crop. Rated excellent for indoor and outdoor containers.*
Carrots are probably a near-perfect plant for containers. They take little space, they really aren't fussy about temperature (even though they're rated a cool season crop), and they'll stay in the ground a long time without spoiling. You can just go and pull one up any time. In addition, carrots come in a variety of shapes and sizes. You can grow long, slender carrots (Gold Pak, Imperator); medium, fat carrots (Royal Chatenay, Spartan Bonus); middle, slender carrots (Danvers Half Long); short, slender carrots (Little Finger); and short, fat (Ox-Heart).

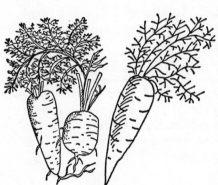

How to Grow. Plant by scattering the seeds across the container surface, roughly 1 inch apart. Cover with about ½ inch of soil. After a few weeks, thin to 2 inches apart (use the young carrots in cooking or eat raw). In large containers, plant half the crop ten days before you plant the other half.

Caution here. If the carrot tip touches the bottom of the pot, the carrot will not develop to maturity. Simply make sure your container is deep enough for the variety you intend to grow.

For indoor containers, plant any time. Outside you should plant carrot seed on the approximate date of the last frost in your area. (See frost map, Chapter 3.) You can then continue to plant up to about sixty days before the first frost of fall. You can grow carrots all summer long except in the hottest areas. If the summer sun is exceptionally hot on the patio (above 90 degrees), provide some shade.

Varieties to Grow

	Days to Maturity	
Very short		
Ox-Heart	65	Short, chunky, does well in shallow pots
Short		
Little Finger	65	Baby carrot, colors quickly, 3½ inches long
Short medium		
Royal Chantenay	70	Broad-shouldered, rich orange
Spartan Bonus	75	6-7 inches long, deep orange
Long slender		
Imperator	75	8-9 inches long; sweet, tender
Gold Pak	76	8-9 inches long; rich orange, needs at least 12 inches of soil

4-Inch Pot Tips. You can grow Little Finger or Ox-Heart in 4-inch pots. Limit the pots to three to six Little Finger carrots, two to four Ox-Heart.

Under Lights. You can easily grow carrots with two 40-watt fluorescent tubes.

Typical Problems. *My carrots cracked badly.* This is a watering problem. If you let the soil dry out and water infrequently, the roots will crack open as they start to grow again.
My carrots didn't come up well from seed. You didn't keep the soil wet during the germination period. Try again.

Harvesting Tips. Start harvesting your carrots as soon as they reach finger size. They're delicious at this stage. Large carrots often become woody.

Cauliflower   *Cool season crop. Rated fair for outdoor containers, poor for indoor containers.*

There are few cabbage family relatives prettier than cauliflower (and boy does it taste great with butter!), although it takes a lot of space.

How to Grow. You can plant one cauliflower plant in a 5-gallon container. Buy your plants from a nursery or start your own. Plant seed in peat pots or foil pans about fifty days before you intend to set them out.

Cauliflower, like other members of the cabbage family, just doesn't like heat. If your summers are at all hot, it is best planted in late summer for fall harvest. If you live in an area of cool summers, plant in the spring. If the weather turns hot as your cauliflower nears maturity, you can keep it from going to flower by putting it inside in a cooler area temporarily or by giving it some sort of shade.

To make the cauliflower white (like the kind you buy in a super-market) since it's naturally green, you will need to blanch the heads by gathering the long leaves around the buds and securing them at the top with a wide rubber band.

Varieties to Grow

	Days to Maturity	
Early Snowball	60	White, deep globular shape
Snow King Hybrid	50	All-America winner, flattish heads
Snow Crown Hybrid	53	All-America silver medal; rounded, pure white heads

How to Use. Plant singly in containers for use on the patio, or group containers together to form a "cauliflower patch."

Under Lights. You can start seedlings under two 40-watt fluorescent tubes. They will grow to transplanting size within eight to ten weeks.

Typical Problems. *My cauliflower heads are small.* Any time the growth stops, you're likely to get undersized heads. Most likely cause—you let the planting mix dry out.

Harvesting Tips. Pick cauliflower as soon as the heads are solid. Don't wait until the bud segments begin to separate to form flower heads.

Corn

Warm season crop. Rated good for outdoor containers, poor for indoor containers.

For some reason, corn always looks tropical when growing on a patio because of the wide, flat leaves. While it takes a lot of space, there's no other vegetable I know of that will make you feel more like a real farmer. In addition, corn is great because you have such a wide choice of varieties.

Container Planting. Plant corn in containers with a soil depth of 8 inches or more. Space plants 4 inches apart, then cover with 1 inch of soil. Plant to grow at least a dozen corn plants close together. The tassels contain the male parts, and the silks that come out of the ears are part of the female flowers. Wind-borne pollen from the tassels of one plant falls on the silks of another plant. Each silk that receives pollen produces a mature kernel. Because the pollen can't float very far, the plants must be fairly close together. And because each kernel is pollinated separately, you must grow only one variety at a time on your patio. Otherwise the varieties will cross-pollinate, and the ears will have mixed kernels.

Corn is a heat lover, so plant the seeds after the patio has warmed up. After that you can make additional plantings every two weeks for a continuous crop.

Corn is also a heavy feeder. Feed supplemental liquid fertilizer every week during the growing season according to the instructions given on the bottle.

Varieties to Grow

	Days to Maturity	
Yellow		
Early Sunglow	63	4-5 feet high, stays tender a long time
Butterfinger	66	Golden yellow kernels, 5 feet high, vigorous in colder weather, especially good for a patio
Earliking	66	Extrasweet, vigorous, 5¼ feet high
Seneca Chief	82	Sweet corn, 5-6 feet high
White		
Silver Sweet	65	6-inch ears, grows to 6 feet
Bicolor		
Honey and Cream	78	5-6 feet high, high yielder

How to Use. Plant a number of plants together in one container, or plant several containers close together on your patio. It is possible to grow corn in one large container indoors behind a south-facing window. This technique is in the experimental stage, but if it sounds interesting, by all means give it a try.

Under Lights. You can start corn under lights, using two 40-watt fluorescent tubes, then transfer them to outdoor containers.

Typical Problems. *The kernels often wind up white, yellow, and other colors on the same ear.* You planted more than one variety close together. A good rule for patio apartment farmers is one variety to each individual patio area.

Harvesting Tips. The sugar in the kernels starts to turn to starch as soon as you pick the ear, causing it to lose its sweet flavor. Therefore, cook corn as quickly as possible after picking. When the silks dry up, slit the shucks, and look to see if the kernels are ready. They should be large and well colored, but not tough. At the best eating stage, juice will spurt when tested with your thumbnail. If the juice is clear, wait. If it's paste, you've waited too long. By the way, you're going to have to figure out how to build a scarecrow yourself.

Cucumbers

Warm season crop. Rated excellent for outdoor containers, poor for indoor containers.

Cucumbers are a natural for patio gardens. They'll do almost anything. You can grow them up a trellis, let them dangle from hanging

containers, run them up balcony railings, and more. In addition, you can tailor the cucumbers you grow by utilizing the proper variety in the first place. Consider size, taste, shape, and color.

Cucumbers are really crazy mixed-up plants. (The first ten to twenty flowers that are produced on each plant are males; after that there are ten to twenty male flowers for every female.) The plants produce many nonproductive flowers (male) before they get down to the business of really making cucumbers (from the female flower), so don't get discouraged that the first few blossoms aren't producing any fruit—they'll be along shortly.

Cucumbers are divided into two families, *white spine* and *black spine*. The spines are miniature stickers that protrude from the warts when fruits are young. White spine cucumbers turn creamy white when completely mature, black spine varieties turn yellowish orange.

How to Grow. Plant regular-sized cucumbers, two to three plants per container in 5-gallon or larger containers. Cover with 1 inch of soil and keep moist. Plant after the days have warmed up in the spring. If you want to get a head start for outdoor planting, plant the seeds ½ inch deep in peat pots two to four weeks before you intend to plant outdoors. Indoors, grow either in a window or under lights.

Varieties to Grow

	Days to Maturity	
For salads		
Improved Long Green	60	8-10 inches long, black-spined
Marketer	65	Extra fancy, 8 inches long, white-spined
Marketmore 70	67	Dark green

For pickles

Spartan Dawn	51	Compact vines, abundance of small pickles
Pioneer	51	Uniform shape, tolerant to disease
Wisconsin SMR 18	54	Warted pickles that brine well

How to Use. Grow cucumbers vertically. Tie the larger cucumbers with 2-inch-wide cloth slings. You can nail a trellis to a large container and run the cucumbers up strings. You can nail a 2-by-2-inch, 6-foot-long post, to the back of a large container, put a 1-by-2-inch cross brace on top, and run the cucumbers up strings. A circle of construction wire can be built as a fence around a half whiskey-barrel. They can be planted in long narrow boxes, and run on strings up a patio wall.

Under Lights. It is possible to grow cucumbers to maturity under lights in winter, but nobody can say it isn't a lot of trouble. You can run the vines on a string close to two 40-watt fluorescent bulbs. You will have to hand-pollinate the blossoms, however, because cucumbers normally need bees to get the pollen from the male to the female flowers. You can buy a blossom set from any garden store, and apply it as a spray (using a perfume atomizer) on the freshly opened female flowers on the miniature cucumbers.

Typical Problems. *My cucumbers are terribly bitter.* Some gardeners believe this is due to uneven watering. Others say it is due to temperature fluctuation. If you're having trouble getting a good-tasting cucumber, try the Marketmore 70. This was developed by Cornell University and is not bitter.

Harvesting Tips. Pick cucumbers before they begin to turn yellow and the seeds harden. Keep picking fruits. Old fruits left on the vines inhibit the formation of new fruits. For sweet pickles, pick them when they are 2 to 3 inches long; for dills, 5 to 6 inches; for slicing, 6 to 8 inches.

Eggplant

Warm season plant. Rated good for outdoor containers.

Here's a real patio show-off and the favorite of many apartment farmers who are looking for a real conversation piece. Eggplant fruits grow on treelike bushes to 2 or 3 feet tall, so it's like growing your own Christmas tree complete with ornaments. Most varieties produce beautiful shiny, plumpish, purple-black fruit. (We'll take up the others in the chapter on novelties.)

How to Grow. Eggplant needs at least 5 to 10 gallons of soil per plant. Eggplants are heavy feeders, so give them two or three additional feedings after the fruits begin to form. Set out transplants in your containers on the patio after the ground has warmed up, if you want to start from seed. Sow the seeds ¼ to ½ inch deep in peat pots eight to ten weeks before you intend to transplant them into regular containers. Seeds take three weeks or more to germinate. Eggplants are heat lovers and must grow steadily and unchecked during the summer. This means the container mix should never dry out.

Varieties to Grow

	Days to Maturity	
Burpee Hybrid Eggplant	70	Tall, semispreading bush
Early Beauty Hybrid	62	Early; short, oval fruits
Black Beauty	83	Fruit about the size of a cup
Burpee's Jersey King Hybrid	75	Spreading bush, purple skin

How to Use. Utilize singly on the patio as a show-off conversation piece, or group together to form an eggplant "orchard."

Under Lights. Eggplants grow exceptionally well under two 40-watt fluorescent tubes at a temperature of 65 to 70 degrees. With enough light, it is possible to get fruit; however, eggplant grows best on the patio. You can start your container early inside under lights, then move outdoors later for early maturity.

Typical Problems. *My eggplants produced only a few fruit.* You starved your eggplant by not feeding it enough nutrients, or you let the soil dry out.

Harvesting Tips. Pick the fruits when they are dark purple and have grown to about 6 inches long. Don't utilize fruit that has reached full size and begins to lose its sheen.

Kale *Cool season crop. Rated good for outdoor containers, poor for indoors.*

This is a beautiful plant used for greens much like spinach that will greatly enhance the appearance of your patio. Individual plants grow 2 or 3 feet high and just as wide. Kale also produces prolifically and will give you sweet greens from about 60 days after you first plant to after the first frost.

How to Grow. Plant kale in 5-gallon or larger containers. Sow seeds three or four to a container and thin to 16 inches apart. Give additional feedings during the season. Kale's affinity for cool weather determines when you plant. If your summers are cool, with an average daytime temperature of 75 degrees or less, plant in the spring. Otherwise, sow seed in midsummer so that the plants grow during the cool days of fall. Light frost greatly improves the flavor.

Varieties to Grow

	Days to Maturity	
Dwarf Blue Curled Vates	60	Low, compact, bluish green leaves
Dwarf Siberian	65	Thick, grayish green plumelike leaves

Under Lights. Kale can be grown to maturity under lights with two 40-watt fluorescent tubes.

Typical Problems. Kale has few problems, except the heat problem mentioned.

Harvesting Tips. Cut the outer leaves as needed. This keeps the plants producing additional leaves all season long.

Cool season crop. Rated excellent for indoor and outdoor containers. **Lettuce**
This is probably the apartment farmer's very best container vegetable. Lettuce is easy to grow, and it will do extremely well in small containers under lights or on the windowsill. You can also plant loose-leaf lettuce between larger, long-maturing plants like tomatoes, zucchini, corn, eggplant, and similar plants in large containers. There are dozens of excellent varieties to select from, but there are basically four types:

Head lettuce requires eighty to eighty-five days to mature and develops fairly tight heads (this generally is the lettuce you buy in supermarkets).

Butterhead matures in sixty-five to eighty days and forms small, open heads.

Loose-leaf matures in forty to forty-five days and separates into individual leaves.

Romaine matures in seventy to eighty days and forms long, lightly folded heads.

How to Grow. You can start lettuce directly from seeds or transplant seedlings. Purchase the plants from a nursery, or grow your own. For planting directly in a container, plant head lettuce 10 inches apart, butterhead 4 to 5 inches apart. With romaine or loose-leaf lettuce, you have a choice. If you expect to pick the outer leaves over a period of time and let the interior leaves grow, then plant 10 inches apart. If you intend to pick the entire plant at once, plant 4 inches apart. Cover with ¼ to ½ inch of soil.

Lettuce will go to seed in hot weather. Thus, if you plant in front of a hot window or on a hot patio, you will need to give the lettuce some protection. Use either a gauze or lath frame. In addition, seeds often will not germinate in warm soil.

Make outdoor plantings at two-week intervals in a large, divided container starting in very early spring, or plant every two weeks in individual 6-inch pots. Indoors, you can plant lettuce any time. You can also plant in large containers in the dead of winter. Bring the plants to maturity under lights, then move them outdoors. Be sure to thin without mercy to the required spacing.

Varieties to Grow

	Days to Maturity	
Head lettuce		
Great Lakes	90	Slow to go to seed, stands up in warm weather; good quality heads
Penlake	72	Uniform head
Burpee's Iceberg	85	Compact heads, leaves savoyed (crinkled)
Butterhead		
Butter King	70	Large butterhead, heat-resistant
Buttercrunch	75	Compact and heavy
White Boston	80	Solid heart, blanched to bright, creamy white
Loose-leaf		
Oakleaf	45	Heat-resistant; leaves shaped like oak leaves
Salad Bowl	50	Crinkly leaves, heat-resistant
Slobolt	45	Heat-resistant, slow to go to seed; crisp leaves
Early Prizehead	45	Tender loose heads; bright green leaves
Romaine		
Paris Island Cos	76	Firm heads 10 inches high; heat-resistant
Paris White Cos	83	Heat-resistant; light-green leaves

How to Use. Place one plant (loose-leaf varieties) in a 4-inch pot. Harvest the leaves whenever you need them. You can grow separate paper pulp pots of lettuce on the patio, grow in window boxes, set out in 6-inch pots on patio wall shelves, or plant an entire grow-light garden with different kinds of lettuce.

4-Inch Pot Tips. You can grow any loose-leaf lettuce in a 4-inch pot, one plant to a pot. Heads take about six to nine weeks when started from seedlings.

Under Lights. Lettuce grows rapidly under two 40-watt fluorescent tubes. The plants grow so rapidly, however, that you must feed once a week to avoid a nitrogen deficiency. If lettuce needs supplemental feeding, it will tell you by turning yellow.

Typical Problems. *My lettuce turns brown at the tips.* It gets much too warm during the summer for lettuce on a south- or east-facing patio or behind glass. It is best to plant for early spring and late fall harvests, or give the lettuce partial shade by hanging a bamboo shade with every other slat removed over the window.

Harvesting Tips. Harvest head lettuce when the center feels firm.

Warm season crop. Rated fair for outdoor containers, poor for indoor containers.

Melons

On first glance, you'd think melon vines would take up far too much space to ever grow in an apartment. But that isn't at all true. Watermelons may be impractical (although I have one friend who grows the biggest watermelons I've ever seen six stories above the street), and you may want to limit yourself to the muskmelons and the midget watermelons (which we'll discuss in Chapter 9). The real trick is not to let the vines take up patio space, but make them grow up in the air on some sort of structure.

How to Grow. Grow melons in 5-gallon or larger containers, two plants per container. Melons are heavy feeders, so give one or two supplemental feedings during the growing season. To get a jump on the season, plant seed indoors in individual peat pots six to eight weeks before you expect to move them outside. You can plant seedlings outside after the days have warmed up. In addition, you can plant the early maturing varieties in short summer areas.

Varieties to Grow

	Days to Maturity	
Hearts of Gold	90	Orange flesh, round, 5 inches across
Honey Rock	85	Deliciously sweet, almost round
Samson Hybrid	90	Sweet tasting; deep-orange flesh

How to Use. Put construction wire around the top of a large planter, and as the vines grow tie them to the wire with string or twisters. Utilize two or three planters in front of a wall, and grow the vines on wires up the wall. Support the fruit with 2- or 3-inch cloth strips tied to the cross wire.

Under Lights. Melons grow well under two 40-watt fluorescent lights initially. Plant in peat pots, and transfer the seedlings when they are 2 to 3 inches high into your regular patio containers.

Typical Problems. *My melons taste bitter.* Bitterness can occur because of wet, cold weather during the ripening period. Melons need warm weather to do their best and a small scoop of ice cream in the center to taste their best.

Harvesting Tips. Cantaloupes are ready to eat when the stem slips off easily. The opposite end of the plant also softens, and the netting becomes thick and corky as the plant ripens. For Persian and crenshaw, sniff the blossom end. If it smells fruity and sweet, the melon is ready. The casaba is ready to pick when the rind has turned deep-yellow.

Cool season crop. Rated excellent for indoor and outdoor containers. **Mustard Greens**

This is a great vegetable for apartment farms. Long a Southern favorite, it is used for cooked greens and in salads. Mustard reaches maturity rapidly (thirty-five to forty days) and therefore can be used for intercropping in big containers between larger, slower-growing plants.

How to Grow. Sow seeds about 2 inches apart, and cover with ½ inch of soil. Later thin to 4 inches apart. Sow the seed early in the spring and again late in the summer. You can also sow inside during the winter for under lights or windowsill harvest, as long as you keep the temperature below 70 degrees.

Varieties to Grow

	Days to Maturity	
Florida Broad Leaf	43	Smooth leaves, broad
Southern Giant Curled	40	Fringed, bright green
Tendergreen	35	Dark-green leaves, rapid-growing

How to Use. Indoors or outdoors plant in any size container from 4 inches up. Hang in 12-inch pots under the eaves. Place 12-inch paper pots of mustard on patio wall shelves.

Under Lights. Mustard greens grow to maturity under two 40-watt fluorescent tubes in about thirty-five days.

Typical Problems. *The minute it turns warm my plants start to go to flower.* Mustard is a cool weather crop. Once flowering starts, nothing helps, not even snapping off the tops. You simply must wait until cooler weather and put in new plants.

Harvesting Tips. Take off the outer leaves as you need them.

Okra *Warm season crop. Rated fair for outdoor containers, poor for indoor containers.*

Okra can be a really delicious addition to your balcony or patio. It adds a real flavor to soup stock or seafood gumbos. The plant itself is fairly large and erect and has a distinctly tropical look.

How to Grow. Plant one plant to each 10-gallon or larger container. Soak the seed overnight in a pan of water, then cover with ½ to 1½ inches of soil. Place outdoors on the patio only after the days have warmed up to 65 degrees or more.

Varieties to Grow

	Days to Maturity	
Red River	70	Tropical look, good yields

How to Use. Grow singly in a large tub on the patio. Use to create a tropical motif. (It's related to the hibiscus.)

Under Lights. Okra can be started as seedlings under lights in peat pots, then transferred to outdoor planters after a few weeks.

Typical Problems. *I live in an area of cool summers, and my okra doesn't do very well.* Okra needs heat. It is not a good plant for cool summer areas.

Harvesting Tips. Harvest pods with a paring knife when they are 1 to 3 inches long. They can be tough if allowed to go past their prime.

Onions *Cool season plant. Rated good for indoor and outdoor containers.*
Onions are a universal vegetable that everybody loves, unless you tell people about them right after tasting your yield. You can grow them into mature onions in large containers on the patio. Personally, I prefer to grow only small pots of green onions for use in salads, since it takes a long time to get good onion bulbs. You can buy special varieties

of scallions or green onions. I don't recommend them, however, since they take so long to mature. Simply plant regular onion varieties and harvest during the young, tender, green stage (about thirty-five days after planting).

How to Grow. You can grow onions from seeds, seedlings, or sets (small bulbs or roots).

Seeds should be planted about 1 inch apart and covered with ¼ inch of soil. Keep moist. They will grow fine as green onions on 1-inch spacing. For bulbs, thin to 3 inches apart (you will need about 12 inches of soil depth). Use the thinned plants as green onions.

Seedlings purchased from a nursery should be planted 1 inch apart and then thinned to 2 to 3 inches apart as they grow larger.

Sets are probably the best way to grow onions because they are easy to handle, although the variety of onions you can purchase as sets is limited. Plant sets 1 to 2 inches apart.

Onions grow above the ground in cool weather, below the ground during warm weather. They need a lot of moisture, so never allow the soil to dry out. Since onions like cool weather, seeds, seedlings, and sets should be planted on the patio in early spring. You can plant all winter long in areas that have mild winters. For windowsill planting, follow the patio schedule. Under lights, plant any time but keep the temperature for green onions between 60 and 70 degrees.

Varieties to Grow

	Days to Maturity	
White Sweet Spanish	110	Very large, globe-shaped
Southport Yellow Globe	65	Good quality white, fine green
Southport Red Globe	100	Thick, purplish red

How to Use. Grow indoors either under lights or on the windowsills as green onions. Grow outside in larger containers for bulbs. Utilize a patio wall or window wall-shelf for pots of green onions. Hang green onions in a window.

4-Inch Pot Tips. Plant a bunch 1 inch apart for windowsill use. Harvest in about thirty-five to forty days for green onions.

Under Lights. You can start all onions quite successfully under two 40-watt fluorescent bulbs. Long hours of lamplight encourage onion seedlings to grow as spring onions. Ten to twelve hours of lamplight daily encourages bulb formation.

Typical Problems. *My onions didn't become very big.* Either you didn't thin enough (apartment farmers hate to thin), or you didn't keep the soil moist. The soil shouldn't dry out while bulbs are forming.

Harvesting Tips. Start thinning the green onions as soon as they're big enough to make it worth while. For bulbs, when the tops begin to dry and yellow, bend them over to a nearly horizontal position on the ground and break them off. This will divert all growing energy to the bulbs. When all the tops are dead, dig up the bulbs with a large kitchen spoon, then let them dry out on a newspaper in a windowsill.

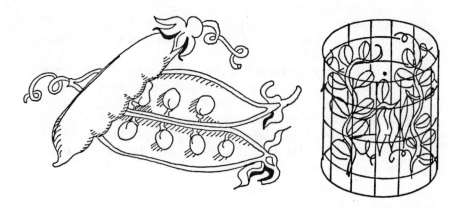

Peas   *Cool season crop. Rated fair for outdoor containers, poor for indoor containers.*

If you want a good reason to plant peas, just remember the mouth-watering flavor of young tender peas smothered with butter— Wow! Peas normally take a lot of space for the crop produced. However, you can increase the quantity by planting the taller pole varieties along a patio wall or up construction wire nailed to the back of a long planter box. For fun, though, you should try the lower-yield but faster-maturing dwarf varieties, which also are quite decorative. Peas are a cool season crop that comes up well in the spring, when the days are cool and moist. They will produce well into the warmer days, but should not be started during the hot days of summer.

100

How to Grow. Plant in 5-gallon or larger containers. Peas do best in long planter boxes along a wall. Plant 2 inches apart, add 2 inches of soil, and keep moist. Plant seeds on the patio in early spring two to three weeks before the last killing frost. (See frost map, Chapter 3.)

Varieties to Grow. Generally, two kinds of peas are grown in apartment farms: common green peas, raised for their edible seeds, and sugar peas (Chinese snow peas), raised for edible pods.

	Days to Maturity	
Tall		
Alderman	74	High quality peas, grows 4½-6 feet long
Medium		
Wando	68	Productive hot-weather pea, tolerance for heat and cold, 2½ feet long
Alaska	55	2½ feet long
Edible-pod peas		
Dwarf Gray Sugar	65	2-2½ feet long
Small		
Little Marvel	63	Dark green, 1½ feet long
Green Arrow	70	High yield, 2 feet long

How to Use. Plant in a half whiskey-barrel, put up a construction wire circle, and train peas up the wire. Or plant in long container boxes along a wall. Because of the quantity of vines necessary for a good pea crop, probably the preferred way of growing is to grow peas on chicken wire.

Under Lights. Peas go wild under lights, but because of the quantity of vines required, they are impractical to grow as a crop.

Typical Problems. *My vines are green and bushy but produce few peas.* To start producing peas, pinch back the growing tips.
My pods are hard. You're letting them stay on the vines too long.

Harvesting Tips. Start picking when pods have swelled to an almost round shape. Pick every few days. Pick sugar peas when pods are 2 to 3 inches long and the pods are undeveloped. Don't let overmature pods remain on the plants, as this cuts down on the total yield.

Peppers   *Warm season crop. Rated excellent for outdoor containers, fair for indoor containers.*

What a plant for the apartment farmer! I love them because of their attractive appearance and the fact that they are so versatile on the patio. There are two major types, sweet and hot. Sweet peppers vary from yellowish green to bright yellow to red when ripe. Hot peppers are generally shiny yellow to shiny, bright red. And needless to say, hot, hot, hot!

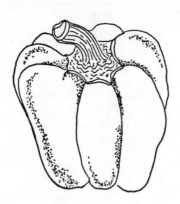

How to Grow. Plant peppers in 2-gallon or larger container. Buy pepper plants from a nursery for transplanting. Peppers are hot-weather plants and like temperatures above 60 degrees and below 90; fruit doesn't set well above or below these limits. If you want to grow your own seedlings, start seeds indoors in peat pots, two to four seeds ½ inch deep, ten weeks before you intend to plant in containers. Peppers need a lot of watering and fertilizing.

Varieties to Grow

	Days to Maturity	
Sweet peppers		
Bell Boy Hybrid	75	Block-shaped
California Wonder	75	Stuffing pepper
Golden Calwonder	72	Large fruits, golden-yellow at maturity
New Ace Hybrid	68	Short bushes, pendant fruits
World Beater	73	Dark green, turning to deep red
Yolo Wonder	76	Large fruit, a standard
Hot peppers		
Anaheim M	77	Long tapered, pungent
Long Red Cayenne	72	5 inches long, curled and twisted

How to Use. Grow peppers singly or in groups in large patio containers. By all means also try one or two peppers in 12-inch pots behind a south- or east-facing window.

Under Lights. Start seedlings under two 40-watt fluorescent tubes.

Typical Problems. *My peppers don't form well.* As mentioned, blossoms don't set well below 60 degrees and above 90. Also, dry container soil can inhibit pepper formation. In addition, overripe peppers left on the vines reduce the yield.

Harvesting Tips. Clip off the peppers as soon as they reach usable size or turn their mature color. Most apartment farmers believe peppers reach their best flavor picked green, not red. Let hot peppers mature on the plant.

Potatoes

Cool weather crop. Rated fair for outdoor containers, poor for indoor containers.

Some people say potatoes aren't a good container crop because they take so long to mature and have such a wide-spreading root system. But why let them grow to maturity? I've found small, immature, container potatoes just delicious, especially with butter. And you can churn out fifty to one hundred small potatoes in a 5-gallon container.

How to Grow. Buy potato sets (seed pieces) from a local nursery, or order from a seed catalog. You can also buy potatoes from a supermarket and cut them into chunks, although unfortunately many are treated with a sprout inhibitor to keep them from growing. Cut pieces about 1½ inches square. Make sure you have one good eye in each piece. (The upper portion becomes the top, the lower portion the roots.) Bury about 6 inches apart, 4 inches deep, cut-side down, in your containers; four or five to a 5-gallon container. Plant in early spring. In mild winter areas, plant in July for a winter harvest. Start pulling the first small potatoes when they are about 1 to 2 inches long. Let the others grow a bit, but never let them grow beyond 2½ to 3 inches. Keep moist.

Varieties to Grow

	Days to Maturity	
Kennebec	60-70	White
Norland	60-70	Smooth red skin

Also ask your nursery for recommended varieties.

How to Use. Grow in 5-gallon or larger containers on patios. Try one or two behind a window. Can be grown under lights as a foliage plant.

Typical Problems. Few, if grown according to instructions.

Harvesting Tips. Pull up individual plants in their entirety. Do not try to harvest potatoes individually.

Radishes

Cool season crop. Rated excellent for indoor and outdoor containers. Radishes are really the apartment farmer's vegetable since they ignore amateur mistakes, and they mature rapidly. I especially like them because of their variety. They run, for instance, from round red, to one-third white, to two-thirds white, to all-white round and all-white long. Just take your pick.

How to Grow. You can easily grow radishes in a 4- to 8-inch soil depth. Plant seeds 1 inch apart, then add ½ inch of soil on top. Keep moist. Sow in indoor containers any time, sow outdoors in patio containers two to four weeks before the last killing frost. (See frost map, Chapter 3.)

Varieties to Grow

	Days to Maturity	
Ordinary radishes		
Cherry Belle	22	Round cherry-sized, smooth, red
French Breakfast	23	Red-white tip
Sparkler	25	Red top, lower third white
Burpee White	25	White, nearly round
White Icycle	28	White, 5 inches long, slender
Winter radishes		
White Chinese	60	Pure white, 6-8 inches long
China Rose	52	7 inches by 2 inches; hot, crisp

How to Use. Use 4-inch pots, both indoors and out. Grow on shelves under fluorescent lights. Grow in hanging pots. Make a salad-garden tree on your patio, using two 4-by-4-inch posts with small pot shelves. Grow pots of radishes at different levels.

4-Inch Pot Tips. Grow four to five radishes per 4-inch pot.

Under Lights. You can grow radishes very quickly under two 40-watt fluorescent tubes. Grow just like outdoors.

Typical Problems. *My radishes are too hot.* You let the soil dry out. Keep it moist.
My radishes are pithy. Summer-grown radishes turn pithy rapidly. Try giving them some shade.

Harvesting Tips. Begin pulling radishes as soon as they are about the size of a small marble. Discard radishes that are pithy.

Rhubarb

Cool season crop. Rated fair for outdoor containers, poor for indoor containers.

You'll love rhubarb as a patio ornamental because of its huge, crumpled, tropical-looking leaves, although you have to wait two years after planting to begin pulling stalks for eating. Rhubarb dies back or goes dormant each fall and shoots up new leaves in the spring. The plant doesn't do well in extremely mild winter areas. You can, however, achieve dormancy by cutting back on water for several weeks after the plant has stopped producing stalks.

How to Grow. A rhubarb plant needs a minimum of 10 gallons of soil. Purchase rhubarb crowns (roots) from your local nursery for planting in your containers. Dig a small hole with a large kitchen spoon. Set the plants so that the tops of the roots stand 3 to 4 inches below container-mix level. Cover with soil. In two years you can pull stalks for eating.

Varieties to Grow

MacDonald	Brilliant red stalks
Valentine	Deep-red stalks
Victoria	Green rhubarb stalks

How to Use. Plant in a large container, and use as a decorative patio show-off.

Under Lights. Rhubarb generally isn't grown under lights.

Harvesting Tips. Snap off stems at the base with a sideways twist when they are 12 to 18 inches long. Trim off and discard all of the leaf blades. Leave a few stalks on each plant to rebuild the energy in the crown.

Spinach

Cool season crop. Rated good for outdoor and indoor containers.

Spinach is one plant every apartment farmer loves, a fast-growing though short-lived plant that matures in six or seven weeks. Inside, you can grow spinach without difficulty if you can give it a cool room. Outside, it prefers cool weather and needs to be grown rapidly to form those large, luscious-looking leaves.

New Zealand spinach is a good spinach substitute for container gardens. It is not a true spinach, but a low-growing, spreading ground cover that resembles spinach. You can cut the young, tender stems and leaves all summer long. Seeds can be started indoors under lights or outdoors directly in the containers. To start seedlings, sow seeds in peat pots 1 inch deep, then transplant to larger containers. Don't move outdoors until the last frost has passed. (See frost map, Chapter 3.)

How to Grow. Spinach is a good crop for containers and can be grown in 4-inch pots. Sow seeds about 2 inches apart. Cover with ½ inch of soil, then thin seedlings to about 5 inches apart in larger containers. Make at least two plantings ten days apart for a continuous crop. Plant spinach early in the spring and during early fall for windowsill and outdoor containers. You can plant any time for harvesting under lights. Feed a supplemental liquid fertilizer every week according to instructions.

Under Lights. Spinach grows extremely well under two 40-watt fluorescent tubes. By keeping the temperature between 50 and 65 degrees, you can grow and harvest spinach any time.

Typical Problems. *My spinach goes to flower rapidly.* Spinach doesn't take long days and warm temperatures well. You can plant under lights inside if you keep the temperatures down. Or, if you live in mild winter areas, plant in late summer on the patio for a fall crop.

Harvesting Tips. Cut off the outer leaves as you need them. When the first flower bud starts to form, harvest the entire plant immediately, rather than let the spinach go to seed and waste all the leaves.

Varieties to Grow

	Days to Maturity	
Long Standing Bloomsdale	48	Heavy yielder, crinkly; slow to go to seed
Winter Bloomsdale	45	Hardy, resists going to seed, dark green
Hybrid No. 7	42	Crinkled, upright

Squash

Squash takes on a million shapes and really provides huge quantities of food in a small space. My favorite is zucchini, and I probably harvest twenty to forty individual zucchini from each plant. As a result, I have collected zucchini recipes for cookies, casserole dishes, relish, puddings, meat stuffers, and everything else. But I still wind up every season giving part of my crop away. Every apartment farmer should try at least a few squash.

Squash is generally divided into summer and winter squash. Summer squash usually grows on bushy, rather compact plants. The fruits are reasonably small with fairly thin skins. Winter squash has thick skins (shells) and huge vines. While I suppose it's possible to grow winter squash in an apartment, I highly recommend that you stick to the summer kind.

How to Grow. You can grow summer squash in 5-gallon and larger containers (actually, the larger the better), two plants per container. Plant two or three zucchini plants per container in a half whiskey-barrel. Summer squash is extremely easy to grow, but don't set it outside until the nighttime temperatures stay above 55 degrees.

Varieties to Grow. Summer squash offers tremendous variety. You can select from many shapes and sizes: cylindrical, flat and round, long and slender, and crooked.

	Days to Maturity	
Burpee Hybrid Zucchini	50	Shiny, medium green
Burpee Golden Zucchini	54	Glossy, bright-golden color
Early Golden Summer Crookneck	53	Bright yellow, fruit shaped like a gourd

| Early Prolific Straightneck | 50 | Creamy yellow fruits |
| Early White Bush Scallop | 54 | Round fruit with scalloped edges, pale green to creamy white |

How to Use. Grow bush type in large containers or tubes. Grow vine types up a trellis attached to the planter or a wall. Grow on construction wire around the planter. Tie vines to cross wires. Tie fruits to cross wires with 3-inch-wide cloth strings.

Under Lights. Squash grows rapidly under artificial lights, but must be transplanted. Keep the temperature between 65 and 75 degrees.

Typical Problems. *My first, small squash always rot.* Squash produces female flowers before the male flowers are available to pollinate them. These unpollinated "fruit" will simply rot. Before very long, male flowers will show up, and shortly after that the female flowers will begin to produce mature squash. Who said plants aren't like people?

Harvesting Tips. Pick scallop squash when small and greenish. Pick summer squash before the skin turns hard. Test with your thumb nail. Pick yellow varieties when they are pale yellow. Try to harvest most summer squash when it is 4 to 8 inches long.

Swiss Chard

Cold season crop. Rated good for outdoor and indoor containers.
Chard is an all-round vegetable crop that should definitely be grown by every apartment farmer. Few vegetables can match Swiss chard for its vigorous growth and production of delicious, big, crinkly leaves and white stalks. You can cook the leaves like spinach and the stalks like asparagus. Plants take strong summer heat, yet will mature within sixty days where summers are cool.

How to Grow. Sow seeds 1 inch apart, cover with ½ inch of soil. Thin plants to 8 inches. Eat the excess plants. You can plant any time for indoor containers. Outdoors, in cold winter areas, plant seeds in the spring about two to three weeks before the final frost. (See frost map, Chapter 3.) In areas where winter temperatures stay above 25 degrees, plant in the fall.

Varieties to Grow

	Days to Maturity	
Fordhoot Giant	60	Dark-green leaves, much curled
Burpee's Rhubarb Chard	60	Wine-red leaves

How to Use. Grow outside in 12-inch and larger containers. Grow in windowsill gardens or under lights.

Under Lights. Chard does extremely well under two 40-watt fluorescent lights.

Typical Problems. Almost none.

Harvesting Tips. Pick the outer leaves before the stems become stringy. Replacement leaves will grow from the center. Never pick all the leaves if you intend to continue the harvest.

Tomatoes

Warm season crop. Rated excellent for outdoor and indoor containers.

Tomatoes do so well in apartment farms that sometimes I think they were invented just for growing by apartment dwellers. A number of varieties seem especially suited for small containers. The smallest is Tiny Tim, a 12-inch plant with cherry-sized fruits. It can be fruited successfully on a windowsill in a 4-inch pot. Small Fry is slightly larger, with clusters of small fruits. It should be staked in a 6- to 8-inch pot or used in hanging baskets. Burpee Pixie Hybrid, 18 inches tall with clusters of small fruit, grows in baskets or 6- to 8-inch containers. Presto Hybrid reaches 24 inches, with 1-inch fruits, when grown in an 8-inch pot. Patio Hybrid grows to about 30 inches with 2-inch fruits, in a 12-inch or larger container. Plant full-sized tomatoes in 5-gallon or larger containers.

Varieties to Grow

	Days to Maturity	
Standard varieties		
Burpee's Big Early	62	Early producer, big fruit, prolific
Early Girl Hybrid	54	Early producer, large clusters of fruit
Burpee's Big Boy	78	Large fruit, many weigh up to 1 lb.
Special container fruit		
Tiny Tim	55	Plants 15 inches tall
Small Fry	52	Marble-shaped red fruit
Burpee Pixie Hybrid	52	Grows 14-18 inches tall
Presto Hybrid	55	24 inches tall, 1½-inch fruit
Patio Hybrid	55	30 inches tall
Basket Pak	72	1½-inch fruit
Red Cherry	72	7/8-inch fruit

How to Grow. You can start your tomatoes from seeds or buy them as seedlings. I generally always buy my plants from a nursery, but you will have to grow from seed if you want a wide choice of varieties. To start from seeds, plant them ½ inch deep in compressed peat pots. Plant windowsill or grow-light tomatoes any time. For outdoor container planting, don't move seedlings outdoors until the weather has warmed up. To transplant, set tomato seedlings about 12 inches apart if you have a bushy plant. Buy the seedling so that one-half to three-quarters of the stem, as well as the root ball, is below the soil level. Roots will form along the buried stem. For long-stemmed plants, you want three-quarters of the stem underground. Don't place the root ball too deep—only about 4 or 5 inches. This means you will often have to put the root ball on its side. As the plants grow, start pruning out the little shoots that appear between the main stems and the branches. Simply snip out with scissors. You can prune down to a single stem or a couple of major stems. Tie to stakes or to construction wire around the container.

111

4-Inch Pot Tips. Tiny Tim does well in a 4-inch pot in either an east or south window. Pinch the tip buds back to make it branch.

Under Lights. You can start tomatoes with two 40-watt fluorescent units. To grow to maturity and fruit, however, you will need four to six 40-watt fluorescent tubes. Make sure the soil is always moist, fertilize twice a week, and keep at a temperature of 70 to 75 degrees.

Typical Problems. *I have flowers but no fruit.* It's probably still too cold. Tomatoes will pollinate above 60 degrees. Below this, you should probably treat with fruit-setting hormones.

I have rot on the end of my tomatoes. This is blossom end rot, usually caused by sudden moisture shortage in the soil. Make sure your containers are not alternately wet and dry.

Harvesting Tips. Pick tomatoes at the stage they appeal to you. You can also pick when they show just a touch of red, and store them in a warm place to allow them to ripen.

Turnips and Rutabagas

Cool season crops. Rated good for outdoor containers.

Both turnips and rutabagas produce huge crops in larger containers. While they are first cousins and look much alike, there are some differences. Turnips have white flesh, are about 2 inches across, and have purple tops. Rutabagas have white or yellow flesh, are 4 or 5 inches across, and have purple tops. You can cook the leaves of turnips as edible greens.

How to Grow. Sow seeds about 1 inch apart, then thin turnips later to 2 inches apart, rutabagas to 6 inches apart. Plant turnips in midsummer for fall patio or balcony crop. Where winters are frost free, plant in the fall. Turnips mature in about thirty-five to sixty days, rutabagas in about 90 days.

Varieties to Grow

	Days to Maturity	
Turnips		
Early Purple Top Milan	45	Flattened roots, 3-4 inches across
Tokyo Cross	35	Smooth, pure white
Purple Top White Globe	55	Firm, crisp
Rutabagas		
Burpee's Purple Top Yellow	90	Best for table use

How to Use. Grow in standard containers.

Under Lights. Rutabaga can be brought to maturity under lights. Use 12-inch pots.

Typical Problems. Practically none.

Harvesting Tips. Pick greens while they are the size of your hand or smaller; older leaves and stems get stringy. Begin pulling turnip roots when they reach 2 inches in diameter.

CHAPTER NINE

Midget Fruits
and Vegetables

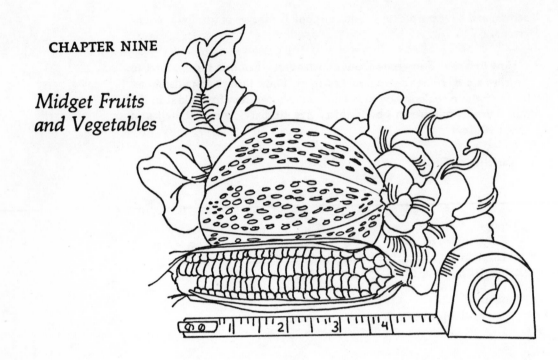

If I didn't know better, I'd say that plant breeders developed the whole range of midget vegetables just for apartment farmers—and they really outdid themselves. Over the last few years a number of vegetables have been developed that are only *half*, even a *fifth*, the size of the regular ones. Thus, you can grow certain fruits and vegetables—watermelon, for instance—that you'd never be able to squeeze into your living area otherwise.

You can grow many of the midget vegetables both indoors and out. It is almost impossible to grow 6- to 8-foot-high corn behind a window, but you can do it with 3- to 4-foot-high corn.

Midget vegetables also mature earlier—generally ten to fifteen days earlier than the larger vegetables. Mini-cantaloupe, for instance, matures in sixty days, compared to ninety days for the typical, larger variety. This allows us to pick sooner, beat the seasonal patio conditions more easily, and, in some cases, harvest a double crop during the same season—a real bonus for apartment farmers short of space.

**How to Grow
Midget Vegetables**

Generally, growing midget vegetables is like growing regular-sized vegetables, but there are some significant differences. You can, for instance, grow most midget vegetables in 4 to 6 inches of soil. This means you can easily grow the larger vegetables in 6-inch pots, the smaller ones, such as carrots, in 4-inch pots.

You must, however, water midget vegetables more often (once a day), since vegetables grown in smaller pots dry out faster. Always check the soil moisture to a depth of 1 inch by poking your finger into the container soil, and if the soil is damp, don't water. (In hot dry weather, check twice a day.)

In addition, the more you water, the more you leach nutrients, so you will need to provide supplemental nutrients to midget vegetables often. Feed a liquid fertilizer containing at least 4 percent phosphorus every two weeks for large containers (8-inch pots or larger), once every week and a half for small containers (6-inch pots or smaller). Mix according to instructions on the bottle.

Now let's look at the individual midget vegetables and where to order seeds for them (addresses are given in appendix).

Cabbage

Dwarf Morden is a good midget cabbage for apartment farms. It has firm, round, 4-inch heads that are sweet, tender, and small enough for close container planting. It takes fifty-five days to maturity. Order from George W. Park.

Baby Head Cabbage is a delicious one-meal cabbage which weighs 2 to 3 pounds, has 4-inch heads, and matures in about sixty-six days. Order from Henry Field.

Little Leaguer is a softball-sized cabbage that matures in about seventy-two days and is very good for containers. Order from Gurney.

How to Grow. Start the midget cabbage from seed indoors in aluminum pans or peat pots about six to eight weeks before you intend to plant in containers. For outdoor containers, plant midget cabbage about 5 inches apart. Plant either before or after the hot weather. For windowsills or under lights, plant in 6-inch pots. Keep the temperature between 60 and 70 degrees.

Carrots

Tiny Sweet Carrot is a tiny, 3-inch-long baby carrot that is delicious. The roots are extremely high in sugar content. It takes sixty-two days to mature. Order from George W. Park.

Midget Carrot is a sweet, juicy, 4-inch carrot—tremendous either cooked or raw. It takes sixty-five days to reach maturity. Order from Gurney, and remember it's wise to begin preparing for this feast well in advance.

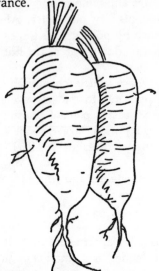

Little Finger is probably the most popular carrot for apartment farmers. This baby carrot colors quickly, is 3½ inches long, and cylindrical with smooth skin. It matures in sixty-five days. Order from W. Atlee Burpee.

How to Grow. Plant six to ten per 4-inch pot. Thin out, and cook smaller carrots. Plant in the spring. Plantings can continue throughout the summer. You can grow carrots in windowsill pots or under lights.

Corn　　*Golden Midget* is a great container corn that grows about 2 to 3 feet high. The ears are 4 inches long, medium yellow, with eight rows of sweet, tender kernels. It matures in sixty-five days. Order from Burgess, Gurney, or George W. Park.

White Midget is a white version of golden midget. It grows 2½ to 3 feet high, and the ears are 4 inches long, with white kernels. It matures in seventy-four days. Order from Burpee.

Midget Sweet corn is extremely tender, flavorful, and sweet. It grows to 2½ feet long, with 4-inch ears, and takes sixty-five days to reach maturity. Order from Henry Field or Gurney.

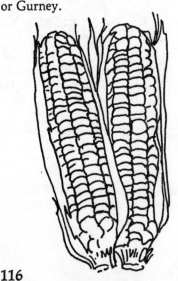

How to Grow. Plant midget corn 5 inches apart in 12-inch or larger pots. Midget corn grows especially well in 5-gallon cans. Plant in the spring after your patio has warmed up. Make additional plantings every few weeks for a continuous harvest. You can also grow 5-gallon containers of midget corn behind a south-facing window all winter long.

Baby Cucumber has bushy vines, matures in fifty-five days, and is very productive. The cucumbers are only 4 inches long. Order from Henry Field.

Little Minnie is ideal for containers. It has vigorous vines that are 2 feet across and bears uniform 4-inch cucumbers. It matures in fifty-two days. Order from Gurney.

Mini Cucumber is a delightful 4-inch cucumber with vines 2 to 4 feet across. It matures in fifty-five days. Order from Gurney.

Tiny Dill Cuke is a midget cucumber that grows on very compact 2-foot vines. It matures in fifty-five days. Order from Burgess.

How to Grow. Plant midget cucumbers in 4- or 6-inch pots, and cover with 1 inch of soil. You can also plant in larger containers, with 4-inch spacing between plants. Place the containers out on the balcony or patio after the days have warmed up in the spring.

Cucumbers

Morden Midget is a sturdy, small, bushy eggplant that bears deep purple fruit. Matures in sixty-five days. Order from George W. Park.

How to Grow. Plant seed ⅓ inch deep in compressed peat pots, and plant pot and all in a 12-inch or larger container. Place in full sun and don't move outdoors until the weather warms up in the spring.

Eggplant

Tom Thumb lettuce is of the butterhead type, with small, firm heads. The leaves are medium-green and crumpled. The centers of the heads are blanched a creamy white. It matures in sixty-five days. Order from Burgess, Henry Field, or Gurney.

How to Grow. Plant midget lettuce directly in your container 4 or 5 inches apart. Midget lettuce grows well in 4-inch or larger pots and is especially popular for window box gardening. Make outdoor plantings every two weeks in separate small containers (or divide a larger one), starting 2 to 4 weeks before the last killing frost in the spring. Inside, plant any time; you can easily grow lettuce on a windowsill or under lights.

Lettuce

Cantaloupe

Melons

Minnesota Midget is a new ´midget cantaloupe that's great for containers. Its small, 3-foot vines produce surprising numbers of 4-inch cantaloupes, with a very high sugar content. The plant takes sixty days to reach maturity. Order from George W. Park.

Watermelon

Petite Sweet is ideal for containers. This is an icebox type melon that weighs 8 pounds, can be held in the palm of your hand, and has a very high sugar content. It matures in sixty-five days. Order from Gurney.

New Hampshire Midget is one of the smallest watermelons, only 6 inches in diameter and 4 to 6 pounds in weight. It is bright red inside and deliciously sweet. It matures in sixty-five days. Order from Burgess.

Lollipop is a sweet and luscious midget watermelon right down to the rind. It matures in seventy days. Order either red lollipop or yellow lollipop from George W. Park.

Golden Midget Watermelon has a built-in ripeness indicator, since it turns a bright, golden yellow when ready to harvest. It is also a convenient size and has a high sugar content. It matures in sixty-five days. Order from Burgess.

Market Midget weighs 3 to 5 pounds, is just right for the refrigerator, and is exceptionally sweet. Matures in sixty-nine days. Order from Gurney's.

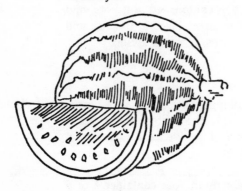

How to Grow. Grow midget melons in 12-inch or larger pots, two plants to a pot, or space in larger containers 10 inches apart. Grow up a trellis or construction wire, and tie the fruits with cloth slings. Melons are warm-weather plants, so move them outdoors after the patio has warmed up in the spring.

Tomatoes   *Midget Tomatoes* are covered in Chapter 8.

That's a quick roundup on the midget vegetables available for the apartment farmer. They are generally easy to grow, suited to your space requirements, and really delicious in the bargain. Give them a try. You'll discover it's a real treat to munch on the munchkins.

CHAPTER TEN

Gourmet Vegetables, Herbs, and Sprouts

The exquisite taste of really fine food often comes from the vegetable world. Herbs, garlic, horseradish, fennel are only a few of the vegetables that impart their own special flavor to cooking. And while all the varied and unusual vegetables used by a good cook can be grown in a normal outdoor vegetable garden, generally such a garden is geared to quantity production of standard vegetables.

However, in your apartment farm it is quite possible to devote an entire window to gourmet vegetables. You can, for instance, plant a container pot each of escarole, cress, herbs, horseradish, and the like. Or you can devote an outdoor container to cardoon, celeriac, and salsify. In your apartment farm you can afford to be more selective, grow smaller quantities, and give them the special attention needed.

Cooking Foreign Foods from Your Apartment Farm

It's always great fun to be able to cook exotic foods, but the problem is that you seldom have all the necessary ingredients on hand. This dilemma is easily solved when you grow the necessary gourmet vegetables right in your own apartment farm. Here are three different combinations you may want to try:

Japanese. Grow soybean sprouts, Garbo (burdock), Daikon, and Japanese eggplant. See the individual vegetables in this chapter for uses.

Chinese. Grow Chinese Cabbage, Chinese white mustard cabbage, chop suey greens, and ginger root.

Italian. Grow Florence fennel, broccoli, chard, green onions, snap beans, zucchini. For herbs, grow basil, marjoram, mint, Italian parsley, summer savory, and garlic.

All of these vegetables are simple and easy to grow. In combination in your apartment farm, they will give you a living pantry you can draw on to create many fine, exotic dishes. No passport or visa is required to enjoy these foreign delights.

Growing Gourmet Vegetables

Vegetable	Cover soil depth (inches)	Spacing (inches)	Germination time (days)	Time to transplanting (weeks)	Time to maturity (days)
Burdock (Garbo)	1/4	2	10-15	-	60-80
Cardoon	1/2	1 per container	8-12	8	150
Celeriac	1/8	8	10-15	10-12	90-120
Chinese cabbage	1/2	12	4-10	4-6	80-90
Chinese white mustard cabbage	1/2	8-12	-	-	80-90
Chop suey greens	1/2	2-3	5-14	-	42
Collards	1/4	10-15	5-9	4-5	70-80
Cress	1/4	2-3	4-10	-	25-45
Daikon	1/2	2-3	-	-	60
Endive	1/2	9-12	5-9	-	60-90
Fennel, Florence	1/2	6	6-17	-	120
Garlic	1	2-4	-	-	90
Ginger	Plant roots	1 per container	-	-	
Horseradish	Plant from division	10-18	-	-	6-8
Japanese eggplant	1/2	1 per container	7-14	6-9	75-95
Kohlrabi	1/2	4	3-10	4-6	60-70
Leeks	1	3	7-12	10-12	80-90
Purslane	1/2	6	7-14	-	
Rocket	1/4	8-12	7-14	-	
Salsify	1/2	2-3	-	-	110-150

In this chapter we will describe some selected gourmet vegetables you can easily cultivate in your apartment, plus several herbs and sprouts. **Gourmet Vegetables**

This plant grows as a weed in many areas, but the root of burdock is edible. The plant itself has long stalks, broad leaves, and sharp burrs. **Burdock**

How to Grow. Plant seed 2 inches apart, ¼ inch deep, in 12-inch pots in the spring. Burdock can also be grown in a windowsill garden in 4-inch pots and under two 40-watt fluorescent bulbs. Sow any time indoors. Keep temperature between 60 and 70 degrees. To harvest, simply pull the roots when needed. Purchase seeds from Nichols Garden Nursery.

How to Use. Burdock (Garbo) is used in many Oriental dishes. You can shave the burdock root into thin slices and saute in oil, then mix with other vegetables. Utilize in any Oriental vegetable dish that strikes your fancy.

Cardoon is in the same family as the artichoke. It is an interesting patio container plant, with deeply cut leaves and a large flower head with purple bristles. **Cardoon**

How to Grow. Start seeds in peat pots, and place each pot in a 5-gallon or larger container. Generally, it is best grown in areas of cool summers, since it is a cool season plant requiring 120 to 150 days to mature from seed. Cardoon is grown for its young leaf stalks. To harvest, cut off the plants just below the crown, and trim the outside leaves. Cut the stalks in pieces, and parboil them in salted water with a bit of lemon juice to prevent darkening. Order from Comstock Ferre and Company, Di Giorgi, Charles C. Hart, Nichols Garden Nursery, or J.L. Hudson.

How to Use. Parboil, then serve cardoon in salads or use as a hot vegetable with butter.

Celeriac is a dark-green form of celery grown for its swollen root and used in many ways by the creative cook. **Celeriac**

How to Grow. Start three seeds to a peat pot in January. When they are about 3 inches high, keep only the most vigorous one in each pot and transplant them to outdoor containers, spaced about 6 inches apart. Order from most catalogs listed in the back of this book.

How to Use. Steam and serve it as a hot vegetable, or shred the raw root and toss it in oil and vinegar.

Chinese Cabbage

Chinese cabbage is an Oriental relative of regular cabbage, with rather elongated compact or loose heads. It is tender, crisp, and sweet.

How to Grow. Plant seeds ½ inch deep, about 8 inches apart, then thin to 12 inches. Indoors, plant any time, but keep out of hot window areas in midsummer. Plant Chinese cabbage to mature in a cool climate, since it quickly shoots up flower heads during the long days of summer. Plant in early spring outdoors in the northern states and western fog belt. Plant elsewhere in midsummer for fall. Order from many of the catalogs listed in the back of this book.

How to Use. Cut in wedges, steam, and serve buttered. Use in coleslaw salad.

Chinese White Mustard Cabbage (Pak-Choy)

This is an interesting Chinese cabbage that resembles Swiss chard, a nonheading type.

How to Grow. Space seedlings 8 inches apart. Grows outdoors or indoors in windowsills or under lights. Plant outdoors in early spring. Order from Nichols Garden Nursery.

How to Use. Good in vegetable or meat dishes.

This grows like spinach and can be purchased in many supermarkets.

Chop Suey Greens (Shunguiku)

How to Grow. Plant 2 to 3 inches apart, ½ inch deep. Harvest when the plants are 4 to 5 inches tall. Order from George W. Park Seed Company and Nichols Garden Nursery.

How to Use. Serve in mixed vegetable dishes.

Collards takes its place along with spinach, mustard greens, and kale, and is the favorite green of many apartment farmers. Collards actually looks very much like lanky, nonheading cabbage. The mature plants often reach 2 to 3 feet in height and resemble kale.

Collards

How to Grow. Sow seeds 5 to 7 inches apart. You can also plant in 4- to 8-inch pots for your windowsill garden or for growing under lights. This is a very hardy plant. It will take a light freeze (down to 22 degrees) and also can withstand the hot days of summer. Indoors, plant any time. Outdoors, plant from spring through to midsummer. Pick collard leaves as they approach full size, before they grow tough and woody. Order from most catalogs listed in the back.

How to Use. Boil the young leaves in salted water, and serve with butter. Many apartment farmers cook collards (Southern style) with ham hocks or salt pork.

Today, cress is being used by many apartment-farmer cooks as a nippy garnish. I recommend mainly the fine, curled cress with the tangy, dark-green leaves.

Cress

How to Grow. Sow seeds in 4- to 8-inch pots for windowsill gardens, and make sowings every two weeks. As an alternative, try growing cress in a shallow tray. Sprinkle seeds on a wet cheesecloth that has been spread on top of potting mix. Keep the cheesecloth moist and stuck to the soil surface. Snip the seedlings in ten to fourteen days. Order from W. Atlee Burpee, Gurney, Nichols.

How to Use. Utilize as a green to garnish salads, sandwiches, roasts, and other dishes. Blend with cream cheese to make a sandwich spread.

Daikon (Oriental Radishes)   These Oriental radishes grow 12 to 18 inches long and taste something like turnips.

How to Grow. Plant seeds in 5-gallon or larger containers in late summer or early spring (for patios). Order from Burgess, W. Atlee Burpee.

How to Use. Add to soup, or grate for use as a garnish.

Endive   Endive is a frilly, somewhat bitter "lettuce" that is actually a member of the chicory family.

How to Grow. Plant about 8 inches apart in outdoor containers, starting in early spring. Plant indoors in 4- to 8-inch pots all year. You need to blanch endive to lessen its bitterness and improve its flavor. Simply draw the outer leaves together at the tips, then tie the bunched leaves together with a string or rubber band. To harvest, remove bruised outer leaves and wash heads under cold water. Order from most catalogs listed in the back.

How to Use. May be used in sandwiches and salads.

Fennel   Florence fennel is grown by apartment farmers for its bulblike base formed by the overlapping leaf stalks. The plant itself is an annual that grows to 2½ feet tall.

How to Grow. Plant 6 inches apart in a large outdoor container. Pull the plant from the ground when the base of the stalk is 3 to 6 inches thick. Harvest the plant when you're ready to use. Order from W. Atlee Burpee.

How to Use. The fennel stalks can be steamed and treated like celery. Utilize raw in salads, or braise as an ingredient in Italian pasta dishes.

Garlic   Garlic is strong medicine in the apartment farm, and many gardeners believe it can be used to control a wide variety of insects. There are two types available: regular garlic bulbs, which contain a number of small cloves, and elephant garlic, which has the flavor of regular garlic but none of its pungency.

How to Grow. Plant garlic cloves 1 to 1½ inches deep, 2 inches apart, base down in full sun in large or small pots. To harvest, dig up the roots when the tops fall over. Order regular garlic from most catalogs. Order elephant garlic from Nichols Garden Nursery.

How to Use. You can slice elephant garlic cloves right into salads, but garlic can be used in all nonsweet dishes.

Ginger

Ginger is cultivated commercially in Hawaii and Jamaica and grows to 3 feet.

How to Grow. Buy some of the knobby root from a supermarket, and plant in a 5-gallon or larger container with the sprout end up. Place out on the patio only after the days have warmed up.

How to Use. After peeling, chop or grate. Use with vegetables.

Horseradish

Horseradish is one gourmet vegetable that should be grown by every apartment farmer, since it can be started so easily.

How to Grow. Buy roots at the supermarket, and place them 1 foot apart in 12-inch or larger patio containers. Set small end up, with the big end 2 inches below the soil surface. Make sure your plants receive plenty of sun. Horseradish has its greatest growth in late summer, so harvest in October and November by pulling up the entire root. Plant inside in a south- or east-facing window. Order from W.

Atlee Burpee, Farmer Seed and Nursery Co., Burgess, Gurney's, and others.

How to Use. Grate fresh horseradish as soon as possible. You can make horseradish sauce by grating the root and blending with vinegar, then mix with beet juice and whipped sour cream. Add grated horseradish to applesauce for an unusual, tart flavor.

Japanese Eggplant   This eggplant has long, narrow fruit and should be harvested when the fruit is two-thirds maximum size.

How to Grow. Eggplant needs at least a 5-gallon container. Eggplants are heavy feeders, so give two to three additional feedings after the fruits begin to form. Set out transplants in your containers on the patio after the ground has warmed up. If you want to start from seed, sow the seeds ¼ to ½ inch deep in peat pots eight to ten weeks before you intend to transplant into your regular containers. Seeds take three weeks or more to germinate. Eggplants are heat lovers and must grow steadily and unchecked during the summer. This means the container mix should never dry out. Order from W. Atlee Burpee.

How to Use. Cook in mixed vegetable dishes. Slice thin, soak in salt water to remove the bitterness, dip in egg batter, and fry.

Kohlrabi   This unusual plant, developed from wild cabbage in northern Europe, looks like a turnip growing on top of the ground.

How to Grow. Plant seed in the spring ½ inch deep in outdoor containers and thin to 4 inches apart. Kohlrabi matures in about two months and may be eaten when the bulbs are 2 to 3 inches in diameter. To harvest, pull them before they are mature. Order from most catalogs.

How to Use. Dice, boil in water, and serve with butter or sauce. Or scoop out large kohlrabi and stuff with ground pork, or cut up and bake. Also use in salads.

Leeks

Leeks look much like a fattened green onion with large top leaves and a small bulb. The flavor, however, is much milder and more delicate than onions.

How to Grow. Sow seeds directly in containers, and thin to 3 to 4 inches apart when about 4 inches tall. Plant inside in 8-inch or larger pots any time. Plant outdoors in early spring. In hot summer areas, sow seeds in summer for winter harvest. As leeks grow, gradually mound loose soil around the stalks to whiten them, keeping the soil surface below the leaf joints. Harvest when they are from ½ to 2 inches in diameter, lifting them with a large kitchen fork. Order from most catalogs.

How to Use. Leeks can be served like asparagus. Boil or braise, and serve with butter or white sauce.

Purslane

In an ordinary garden this is a weed, but in an apartment farm it becomes a delightful delicacy. Purslane grows to 4 inches high and has thick, spatula-shaped, succulent leaves.

How to Grow. Plant indoors in 4- to 8-inch pots any time. Plant seedlings in outdoor containers in the spring about 3 inches apart, then thin to 6 inches. Harvest by picking the leaves when young. The plant will continue producing all season long. Order from Nichols Garden Nursery.

How to Use. Steam and serve as greens with butter, or use as greens in salad.

Rocket

Rocket is another delicious, low-growing, weedlike plant that resembles mustard. It has a strong horseradishlike flavor.

How to Grow. Plant 4 to 6 inches apart, covered with ½ inch of soil. Start in early spring or summer for a fall harvest. Grow indoors in 4- to 8-inch pots any time at about 60 degrees. Order from W. Atlee Burpee and Nichols Garden Nursery.

How to Use. Use leaves in salad.

**Salsify
(Oyster Plant)**

Salsify looks much like parsnip but has a distinctive oysterlike flavor.

How to Grow. Sow the seeds 2 inches apart in the spring in outdoor containers, and cover with ½-inch planter soil. Later, thin to 3 inches apart. Since salsify takes 150 days to mature, you should intercrop with radishes, spinach, lettuce, or Swiss chard in 5-gallon or larger containers. Order from many catalogs.

How to Use. Boil, and serve with bread crumbs or white sauce. Marinate in red wine, dip into light batter, and fry.

Strawberries

This is a favorite of apartment farmers since it's possible to grow a good strawberry crop on the patio. There are actually two kinds of strawberries to grow: the everbearing varieties, which produce crops in the spring and fall, and the June bearing varieties, which bear the year after planting.

How to Grow. Buy plants from your local nursery and plant 10 inches apart in at least a 12-inch pot. Apartment farmers also often grow strawberries in a "strawberry jar," a ceramic vase with pockets for strawberry plants. They must be grown in full sun. In addition, it is important to plant neither too deep nor too shallow. The crown should be just above the soil level. To prevent rot, the topmost roots must be at least ¼ inch below the ground level to prevent drying out. Strawberries withstand light freezes but should be protected against severe weather (cover with plastic).

How to Use. Strawberries can be used in many ways. Ask your local nurseryman to suggest the best variety for your area.

Herbs

Herbs are fun to grow in the apartment farm and are one of the most useful plant groups we can use in cooking. For seasoning, you can almost always use fresh herbs; just pick pieces as you need them.

It's extremely easy to dry herbs in your apartment. Pick the herb, stem and all, wash it, and allow it to drain. Take a clean shopping bag, and spread the herb over the bottom. Hang the shopping bag on a doorknob. After a few days, turn the herb over, then allow it to dry a few more days. Feel with your hand, since any remaining dampness will cause mold to form. Once the herb is dry, crush and bottle in jars with tight-fitting lids.

The plant is an annual with light-green foliage that grows 1 to 2 feet high. It also comes in a bush form.

Basil

How to Grow. Basil will make an attractive plant set in an 8-inch or larger container. Simply sow the seeds about 2 inches apart after the last frost outdoors, any time indoors. To harvest, cut the stems regularly. The more you cut, the more they grow. When the plants flower, cut them about 6 inches from the ground, dry them, then strip the stems and store leaves and flowers in jars.

How to Use. Most Italian cooks would be lost without sweet basil to flavor pasta and other Italian dishes. It's great for almost any other kind of cooking.

Chives are a gourmet's delight, since they can add flavor to so many dishes.

Chives

How to Grow. You can buy pots of chives from a nursery and separate them. Plant a clump in 4-inch pots, or grow them together with other herbs in a larger planter. Plant after the last frost outside, any time inside. Grow in a sunny window or under lights. When you are ready to use it, just clip off what you need.

How to Use. Add chopped chives to such things as salads, soups, eggs, cream cheeses, and sauces.

Dill

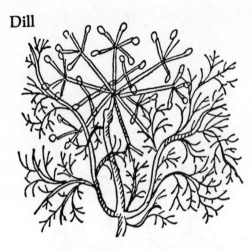

Dill has a very unusual fragrance and a slightly bitter, highly distinctive taste. The plant itself grows 4 feet high, with flowers in clusters.

How to Grow. Sow dill seeds in spring or late summer about 10 inches apart in 12-inch or larger containers. Harvest the seeds from the containers when they begin to turn brown.

How to Use. Use to flavor salads, fish, or lamb.

Marjoram

Sweet marjoram, a member of the mint family, originated in the Orient and, throughout history, has had many medicinal uses.

How to Grow. Sweet marjoram is a bushy plant that grows 1 to 2 feet high. You can grow marjoram in 4-inch or larger pots under lights, on the windowsill (plant any time), or in a sunny part of the patio (when all danger of frost is past). Harvest the leaves and stem-tips at any time, and use them fresh. New leaves and stems will appear after the cuttings. Or pick the leaves just before blossoming. Dry and store.

How to Use. Use as a flavoring for Italian dishes and as an enrichment for salads, casseroles, and veal. Nichols Garden Nursery and Comstock Ferre & Company offer an excellent selection of herbs.

Mint

Probably one of the most useful herbs for the good cook, mint has at least twenty to thirty species, each with its own fragrance and flavor. The distinctive flavors in all mints come from the oils produced within the plants. Spearmint is probably the favorite of most apartment farmers. It grows from 1 to 2 feet high, producing clusters of flowers on a spike. Orange mint grows to about the same height and has a subtle taste. Peppermint grows to 3 feet.

How to Grow. To start mint, plant roots or runners in the spring in 5-gallon or larger containers, or buy a few plants from a nursery. Mint needs lots of water and prefers full sun. To harvest, simply cut a few sprigs whenever you need them. The more often you cut, the better the plants grow. You can also dry the leaves for storage.

How to Use. Serve in ice tea and fruit salads or as a garnish for fresh fruits.

Oregano

A tender perennial, oregano is a close relative of sweet marjoram. It has been an essential seasoning in Latin cooking since ancient times. Today it is found in many Italian, Spanish, and Mexican dishes.

How to Grow. Start oregano from seeds, or buy small plants from a nursery and grow in 4-inch or larger pots. (Replace every two or three years when the plants become woody.) To harvest, pick the leaves as you need them. You can also dry the leaves and store them for later use.

How to Use. Utilize in Italian dishes, or add to lamb and other meats.

Parsley

Parsley is an old favorite that can garnish anything. There are several kinds. Banquet (76 days to maturity) has fine, tightly curled leaves and is ideal for garnishing. Perfection (75 days) is early and vigorous, producing finely curled leaves. Plain Italian Dark Green (78 days) has flat leaves with a strong flavor. Hamburg (90 days) has a root that can be boiled and served like parsnips. Extra Curled Dwarf (85 days) has compact plants, producing five leaves. Plain or Single (72 days) has plain, dark green, deeply cut flat leaves that have a rich, fine flavor.

How to Grow. Sow parsley seeds outdoors in spring or summer. Before planting, soak the seeds in warm water for twenty-four hours to hurry them along, since they're slow to germinate. Sow them 1 to 2 inches apart in a 24-inch pot, and then thin the seedlings to 6 to 8 inches apart. Grow one to two plants inside in a 4-inch pot. To harvest, pick mature leaves whenever you need them.

How to Use. Garnish salads and meat dishes.

Rosemary

Rosemary is a perennial that will live through several years. It can grow to be 6 feet tall, but, fortunately for apartment farmers, there is a dwarf variety. You can grow rosemary outdoors in a 5-gallon or larger container. You can also grow it in a 4-inch pot on your windowsill or under lights, if you keep it trimmed. Propagate rosemary from cuttings taken from a growing plant, or buy small plants from a nursery. To harvest, just cut off the leaves when you need them. When the soil begins to feel dry on top, water well, allow to drain, then don't water again until the top begins to feel dry.

How to Use. Utilize as seasoning for lamb, pork, or veal.

Summer Savory

Summer savory is an annual that grows 18 inches high.

How to Grow. Start summer savory from seed. It is easy to grow outdoors on the patio and in 4-inch pots on your windowsill. Make sure you give summer savory full sun.

How to Use. Flavor salad dressing, fish, and poultry.

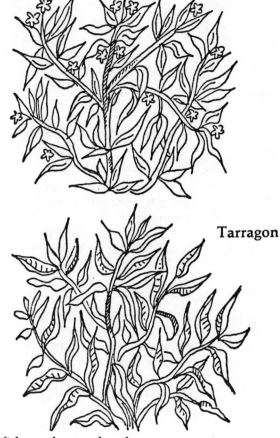

Tarragon

Tarragon is a good seasoning for many foods. It is also a perennial that grows well in the apartment farm.

How to Grow. You can easily propagate tarragon by taking cuttings from existing plants, growing from seed, or buying small plants from the nursery. It grows well in a 4-inch pot indoors on the windowsill or under lights.

How to Use. Use as a flavoring for fish, poultry, and veal.

Thyme

There are many kinds of thyme available; lemon, caraway, golden, French, and more.

How to Grow. You can grow thyme from seeds, start plants from cuttings, or buy small plants from a nursery. It will grow well in 4-inch pots. To harvest, cut plants in full bloom. After they flower, cut plants back to the ground.

How to Use. Use as seasoning for vegetables and meat sauces. Also use to flavor fish, poultry, and veal. Nichol's Garden Nursery and Comstock Ferre & Co. offer an excellent selection of herbs.

Sprouts   One of the great advantages of growing sprouts is that you can harvest your crop in a few days instead of waiting weeks. In addition, this is one type of gardening where you don't have to prepare the soil first.

There are two types of sprouts: the tiny ones that you eat when they form green leaves—alfalfa, cress, chia, mustard, and radish—and the large ones you eat before the leaves open or turn green—lentils, mung beans, wheat, and rye.

Here's how to grow sprouts. First, soak the seeds in water until they are saturated; just a few hours for the small ones, overnight for the larger ones.

To grow, use a small Pyrex baking dish. Sprinkle smaller sprouts on a damp cheesecloth spread on the bottom. Spray the seeds with lukewarm water several times a day and drain. The object is to keep them moist (but not wet) and fairly warm (at least 68 degrees). When the seeds sprout, give them plenty of light (mung beans are the exception—keep these in the dark until ready to use). Use the sprouts in sandwiches, salads, and other vegetable dishes.

Another method is to buy a pint Mason jar and make a lid from a small round screen or cut one from cheesecloth. Soak the seeds as above, and place them inside the jar, with the jar on its side. Keep at 70 to 75 degrees. Spray the seeds with lukewarm water several times a day.

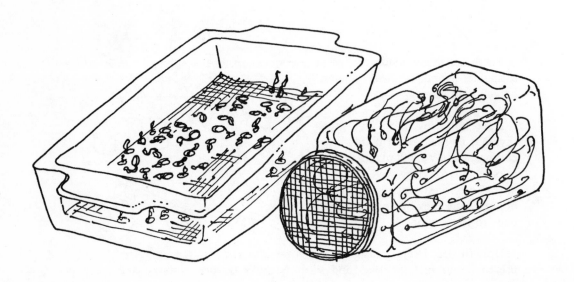

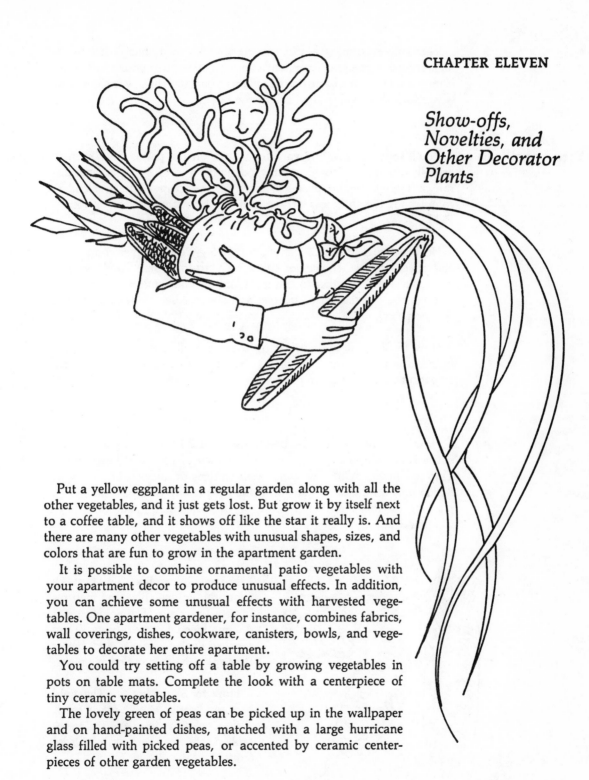

CHAPTER ELEVEN

Show-offs, Novelties, and Other Decorator Plants

Put a yellow eggplant in a regular garden along with all the other vegetables, and it just gets lost. But grow it by itself next to a coffee table, and it shows off like the star it really is. And there are many other vegetables with unusual shapes, sizes, and colors that are fun to grow in the apartment garden.

It is possible to combine ornamental patio vegetables with your apartment decor to produce unusual effects. In addition, you can achieve some unusual effects with harvested vegetables. One apartment gardener, for instance, combines fabrics, wall coverings, dishes, cookware, canisters, bowls, and vegetables to decorate her entire apartment.

You could try setting off a table by growing vegetables in pots on table mats. Complete the look with a centerpiece of tiny ceramic vegetables.

The lovely green of peas can be picked up in the wallpaper and on hand-painted dishes, matched with a large hurricane glass filled with picked peas, or accented by ceramic centerpieces of other garden vegetables.

Vegetable decorating is just coming into its own, but raised to its highest form it can greatly enhance your enjoyment of your apartment. Here are some of the basic novelty plants you can grow. (We show you where to order them in the back of the book.)

Beans—The Yard-Long Bean

You'll love to grow the yard-long bean on the patio. This bean is actually a variety of cowpea with pods up to 4 feet long. The vines are rampant growers and produce an enormous crop of long, slender, round pods the thickness of a pencil. Order from Burgess or Henry Field.

How to Grow. Plant 12 inches apart in 5-gallon or larger containers, and cover with 1½ inches of soil. The yard-long bean needs several months of warm weather to mature. Plant on your patio as soon as the soil temperature reaches 65 degrees and above (check it with a kitchen thermometer).

How to Show It Off. Run it up a patio wall. Make a 2-by-4-foot frame for a 4-foot-long patio planter box. Set at one end of the balcony or patio as a conversation piece.

Beets

How to Grow. Scatter the beet seeds on a 2-inch spacing across the entire container surface. Cover with ¼ inch of soil, and keep moist. Thin to 3 inches apart. For windowsill gardens or under lights, plant in 8-inch pots on the same spacing. Inside, plant any time. Outside, start planting on the approximate date of the last frost. (See frost map, Chapter 3.)

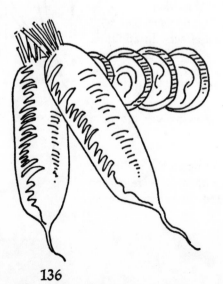

Burpee Golden Beet. This beet is a beautiful, golden color and matures in fifty-five days. The golden roots do not bleed like red beets. They are excellent in salads and better than spinach when boiled as greens.

How to Show It Off. The gold beet can best be shown off as food. Pickle, or utilize in salads and vegetable dishes as a beet novelty. Order from W. Atlee Burpee.

Cylindra Beet. A unique, long, cylindrical beet that will give three to four times the number of slices of a round beet. Roots are dark red and grow 8 inches long.

How to Show It Off. Utilize whole for cooking. Order from Henry Field.

Cabbage— Flowering Cabbage

Flowering cabbage is one of the most beautiful container "vegetables" you can plant (it is not, however, edible). From one planting you can produce as many forms and colors as there are plants, ranging from pink to red to white-on-green.

How to Grow. Plant 10 inches apart in containers. Inside, plant any time. Outside, plant in late July for a fall flowering (flowering cabbage needs cool weather to bring out the colors).

How to Show It Off. Plant in a living room under lights. Utilize in small containers on a patio shelf. Plant several large containers with flowering cabbage. Order from L. L. Olds.

Cauliflower— Purple Head Cauliflower

A real patio show-off. The heads are quite large and deep purple on top. The flavor is almost like that of broccoli, and because of its delicacy, Purple Head is preferred by most apartment farmers.

How to Grow. Plant one cauliflower seedling to a 5-gallon container. You can buy plants from a local nursery or grow from seed. To grow from seed, plant seed in peat pots about fifty days before you intend to set them out. Purple Head, like other cauliflower, doesn't like heat. If you live in an area of cool summers, plant in the spring. If your summers are hot, plant in late summer for a fall harvest.

How to Show It Off. Plant several large containers on a patio. Set off by itself.

Corn

How to Grow. Plant corn in a container with at least 8 inches of soil depth. Space plants 4 inches apart, then cover with 1 inch of soil. Plan to grow at least a dozen corn plants together (we discussed the reason for this in Chapter 8). Corn is a heat lover, so plant the seeds after the patio has warmed up. Feed 1 cup supplemental fertilizer every week.

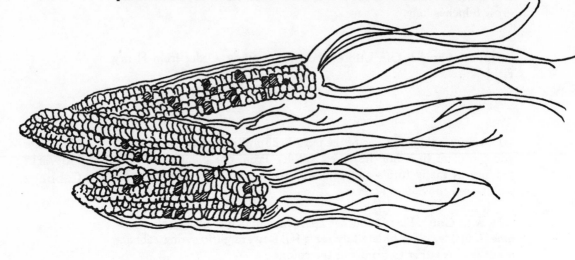

Rainbow Corn. This corn has large ears with kernels in rich tones of deep red, yellow, orange, and blue in endless combinations. Many apartment farmers grow ornamental corn for Halloween and Thanksgiving decorations. This is strictly a decorative corn, and takes 110 days to mature.

How to Show It Off. Harvest and use for centerpieces, cluster arrangements, and similar decorations. Order from W. Atlee Burpee.

Strawberry Ornamental Popcorn. This gets its name from the tiny, 2-inch-long, mahogany-colored, strawberry-shaped ears. It's good for popping, too.

How to Show It Off. Use in floral and table displays. Order from W. Atlee Burpee.

Cucumber   How to Grow. Plant two cucumber plants per 5-gallon container. Cover with 1 inch of soil, and keep it moist. Plant after the patio has warmed up in the spring. To get a head start, plant seeds ½ inch deep in peat pots two to four weeks before you intend to plant outdoors. You can also grow single plants behind a window during the winter.

Armenian Yard-Long Cucumber. Plan to give a good portion of a patio wall to this cucumber. The vine will spread 4 or 5 feet in all directions if you let it. Or instead, grow it up a wood frame, and tie the fruits to the crosspieces with cloth slings. The cucumbers will grow as long as 2½ feet.

How to Show It Off. Give the Armenian Yard-Long a prominent wall where it will get a lot of attention. Order from Burgess.

Lemon Cucumber. This cucumber is a real conversation piece, since it is the size and color of a large lemon with sweet flavor. It takes sixty-five days to reach maturity, and is ready to eat when it begins to turn lemon yellow.

How to Show It Off. Grow in a container on the balcony or patio, and move inside for special occasions. Order from W. Atlee Burpee.

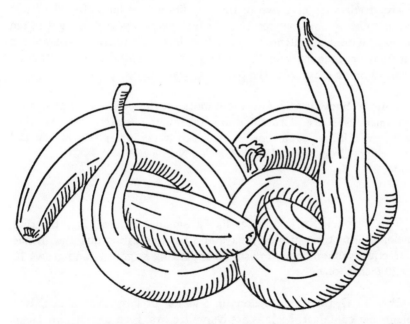

Serpent Cucumber. These long, slim, green fruits sometimes reach a length of 4 feet and coil into realistic snakelike shapes. The taste is very mild, since it doesn't actually belong to the cucumber family. Plant seeds as you would for cucumber, but cover with 1 to 2 inches of soil mix.

How to Show It Off. Grow in a single container in the center of the patio or balcony, and grow the vines up a trellis. Attach the fruits with cloth slings. Order from Burgess.

White Wonder Cucumber. A beautiful, snow-white cucumber that retains the white color when fully ripe. It is a heavy bearer (60 days to maturity).

How to Show It Off. Grow in a container on the patio, and move it inside for special occasions. Order from Burgess.

Eggplant—Golden Yellow Eggplant

This eggplant is a real show-off that produces lemon-sized fruits. The fruit, which takes seventy-five days to reach maturity, has an excellent texture.

How to Grow. Eggplant needs at least a 5-gallon container. They are heavy feeders, so give two to three additional feedings after the fruits begin to form. Sow the seed ¼ to ½ inch deep in peat pots eight to ten weeks before you intend to transplant into containers. Eggplants are heat lovers. Indoors, keep the temperature about 70 degrees. Outdoors, wait to move it out until the patio has warmed up.

How to Show It Off. Grow outdoors on the patio or balcony in a conspicuous space. Grow indoors during the winter in front of a window. Utilize as a coffee table conversation piece on special occasions. Order from Nichols Garden Nursery.

Melons— The Great Banana Melon

This melon looks and tastes like a banana. It is a long, tapering melon that matures in ninety days and has fine eating qualities. It has attractive, salmon-colored flesh, an appetizing fragrance, and grows 18 to 20 inches long.

How to Grow. Grow melons in 5-gallon or larger containers, two plants per container. Melons are heavy feeders. Feed one or two 1-cup supplemental fertilizers during the growing season. Plant seed indoors in peat pots six to eight weeks before you expect to move them outside. Move them outside after the days have warmed up to 65 degrees.

How to Show It Off. Grow in a balcony container, and train the vines up a wall on chicken wire. Be sure to tie the fruit to the wire with cloth slings. Order from R. M. Shumway.

This long, spindle-shaped onion looks like a miniature torpedo. It has a deep purple-red skin and mild, sweet flesh.

**Onions—
Torpedo Onion**

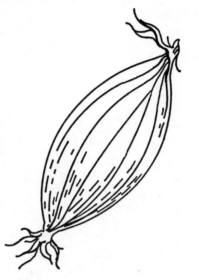

How to Grow. Start from seeds. Scatter the seeds about 1 inch apart, and cover with ¼ inch of soil. Keep the soil moist. Thin to 3 inches apart. Torpedo onions will grow in patio containers or in 6-inch or larger pots inside. Set outside in spring. Onions grow above the ground in cool weather, below the ground during warm weather.

How to Show It Off. Utilize as apartment decorations in a bowl, or string together for wall decorations. Order from Gurney.

This is a real eye-opener, since the Sakurajima radish often grows to the size of a watermelon and weighs 15 pounds. It is round, firm, and crisp, with excellent flavor. It matures in seventy days and tastes good pickled. These radishes are an important food in the Orient. The Japanese slice them, bread them, and fry them in light oil.

**Radishes—
Sakurajima Radish**

How to Grow. Plant on patio in 5-gallon or larger container in summer (to mature in fall) or late fall (to mature in winter).

How to Show It Off. Use them in a decorative table centerpiece. Order from Burgess or Nichols.

The flesh of the fruit of this squash is a spiral of spaghetti-like pulp. when cooked. It is delicious served with hot catsup .or tomato sauce. When fully ripe, the yellow fruit is 8 to 10 inches long. Order from W. Atlee Burpee.

**Squash—
Spaghetti Squash
(Vegetable
Spaghetti)**

How to Grow. Grow in 5-gallon or larger containers, two plants per container. Don't set outside until the night temperatures stay above 55 degrees.

How to Show It Off. Cook and serve on individual plates.

Sweet Banana Peppers

Sweet banana peppers are banana-shaped, 8 inches long, and yellow in color. Actually they progress from light green to yellow to orange, and ripen red. The compact plants bear fruits in great profusion.

How to Grow. Use a 3.5-gallon or larger container (a 12-inch or larger pot). Start seeds indoors in peat pots, two to four seeds ½ inch deep, ten weeks before you intend to plant in containers. Peppers like warm weather, so set outside only after the patio has warmed up.

How to Show It Off. Set a row in containers on the patio, or use in the living room as a conversation piece. Order from W. Atlee Burpee.

In decorating with vegetables, you should constantly be on the lookout for magazine articles that offer ideas. Keep a file of vegetable decorating tips that interest you, and keep trying unusual vegetable combinations.

Allen Sterling & Lathrop, 191 U.S. Route 1, Falmouth, Maine 04105. Listing of varieties and price.

Brecks of Boston, 200 Breck Building, Boston, Massachusetts 02110.

Burgess Seed and Plant Company, P.O. Box 3000, Galesburg, Michigan 49053. This attractive catalog contains special pages on gourmet and novelty vegetables.

W. Atlee Burpee Company, P.O. Box 6929, Philadelphia, Pennsylvania 19132; Clinton, Iowa 52732; P.O. Box 748, 6350 Rutland Avenue, Riverside, California 92502. Burpee maintains three regional offices. The company grows most of the seed it sells. The complete catalog illustrates garden supplies as well as vegetables.

D.V. Burrell Seed Growers Company, P.O. Box 150, Rocky Ford, Colorado 81067. Emphasis on varieties for California and the Southwest.

Comstock Ferre and Company, Wethersfield, Connecticut 06109. A good guide to variety selection.

De Giorgi Company, Inc., Council Bluffs, Iowa 51501. The big catalog features prize-winning seeds.

Farmer Seed and Nursery Company, Faribault, Minnesota 55021. This catalog gives special attention to early maturing vegetables.

Henry Field Seed and Nursery Company, 407 Sycamore Street, Shenandoah, Iowa 51602. The catalog contains a wide selection of vegetables, as well as many garden hints.

Gurney Seed and Nursery Company, 1448 Page Street, Yankton, South Dakota 57078. The catalog emphasizes varieties suited to Northern climates.

Gleckers Seedmen, Metamora, Ohio 43540.

Joseph Harris Company, Inc., Moreton Farm, Rochester, New York 14624. This well designed catalog emphasizes varieties suitable for the northeastern states.

H.G. Hastings Company, P.O. Box 4088, Atlanta, Georgia 30302. Complete southern garden guide.

J.L. Hudson, P.O. Box 1058, Redwood City, California 94604. Catalog has the accent on the unusual.

Jackson & Perkins, Medford, Oregon 97501. This catalog has twelve pages of vegetables.

J.W. Jung Seed Company, Station 8, Randolph, Wisconsin 53956. This catalog contains eighteen pages of vegetables. Emphasis on experiment station introductions.

Kelly Brothers Nurseries, Inc., Dansville, New York 14437.

D. Landrath Seed Co., 2700 Wimarco Avenue, Baltimore, Maryland. America's oldest seed house.

Earl May Seed and Nursery Company, 6032 Elm Street, Shenandoah, Iowa 51601. A complete catalog.

McFayden, P.O. Box 1600, Brandon, Manitoba, Canada. The catalog contains an unusual selection of vegetable varieties especially suited for Northern climates.

J.E. Miller Nurseries, Inc., Canadaigua, New York 14424.

Nichols Garden Nursery, 1190 North Pacific Highway, Albany, Oregon 97321. Specialists in organic gardening; catalog features many unusual vegetable and herb seeds, including French European, and Oriental strains.

L.L. Olds Seed Company, P.O. Box 1069, 2901 Packers Avenue, Madison, Wisconsin 53701. This company puts out an excellent quality catalog.

George W. Park Seed Company, Inc., Greenwood, South Carolina 29646. This long-established Southern nursery offers a large selection of vegetable seeds.

Reuter Seed Company, Inc., New Orleans, Louisiana 70119. Varieties especially for the South.

Roswell Seed Company, P.O. Box 725, Roswell, New Mexico 88201. The catalog emphasizes seeds suited to the Southwest.

Seedway, Inc., Hall, New York 14463. The catalog contains planting instructions.

R.H. Shumway Seedsman, 628 Cedar Street, Rockford, Illinois 61101. This is the kind of catalog you would have expected to receive thirty years ago. It offers many different vegetable varieties illustrated in an old-fashioned and unusual manner.

Stark Brothers Nurseries and Orchards, Louisiana, Missouri 63353.

Stokes Seeds, P.O. Box 548, Main Post Office, Buffalo, New York 14240. The large catalog offers a huge selection of seeds.

Geo. Tait & Sons, Inc., 900 Tidewater Drive, Norfolk, Virginia. Contains planting information for eastern Virginia and North Carolina.

Otis S. Twilley Seed Company, Salisbury, Maryland 21801. This catalog offers many varieties.

The Wetsel Seed Company, Inc., P.O. Box 791, Harrisonburg, Virginia 22801. Sixteen pages of vegetables..

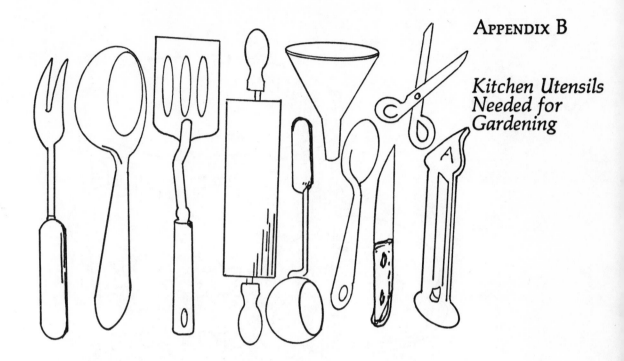

Kitchen Utensils Needed for Gardening

Gardening tools for apartment farming should come directly from your cabinet drawers. Here are a few to try:

Two-pronged metal fork: Use for punching seed holes in transplanted pan soil.

Ice cream scoop: Make equal-sized holes in container soil for transplanting seedlings.

Spatula: Good for moving transplants; can be used to cut transplanting soil into squares.

Small rolling pin: Good for smoothing soil in large containers and transplant flats.

Watering funnel: Place in soil and utilize for watering. This allows water to penetrate to a deeper depth.

Large soup scoops: Use for transferring potting mix into containers.

Paring knife: Good for cutting off side sucker growth in tomatoes and other vegetables.

Small scissors: Use for harvesting chives and similar uses.

Old-fashioned can-opener: Use sharp end for making planting rows in containers and transplant pans.

APPENDIX C

Compost in a Garbage Can

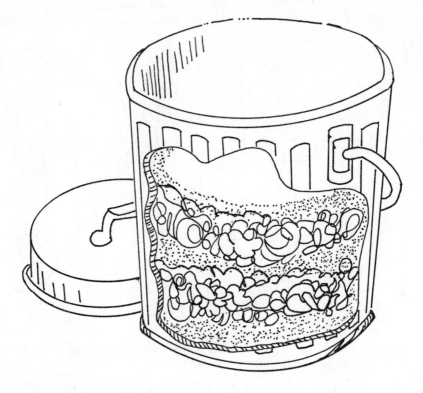

Composting in a small garbage can allows you to utilize good kitchen waste you'd generally just throw away: onion skins, orange peels, spoiled foods, and more. In addition, if it is made right you can have all the compost you need for apartment farming without muss, fuss, or smell. Here are the steps:

1. Obtain two or three 5- to 10-gallon plastic cans with lids. I find mine by asking a painting contractor for his old 5-gallon paint cans. You can also buy small garbage cans from a hardware, discount, or similar store.

2. Buy a sack of sand from your local hardware store and place a 2-inch layer of sand on the bottom of the garbage can or plastic pail.

3. Add a 2- to 3-inch layer of garbage. On top of this place a 1-inch layer of sand. After this, layer the garbage and sand until you reach the top. Keep the lid on top.

4. When the first can is full, start on the next. Good compost takes two to three months.

Atwater, Maxine, *Natural Foods Cookbook.* Concord, Calif.: Nitty Gritty, 1972.

Barnes Jack, *Home Food Drying.* Drain, Ore.: Drain, 1975.

Claiborne, Craig, and Virginia Lee, *The Chinese Cookbook.* Philadelphia: Lippincott, 1972.

D'Agostino, Giovanna, *Mama D's Homestyle Italian Cooking.* New York: Golden Press, 1972.

Dole, Louise E., *Herb Magic and Garden Craft.* New York: Sterling, 1973.

Douglas, James Sholto, *Beginners Guide to Hydroponics.* New York: Drake, 1972.

Dragonwagon, Crescent, *The Bean Book.* New York: Workman, 1972.

Dragonwagon, Crescent, *Putting Up Stuff for the Cold Time.* New York: Workman, 1972.

Elbert, George, *Indoor Light Gardening Book.* New York: Crown, 1972.

Fox, Helen, *Gardening for Good Eating.* New York: Macmillan, 1973.

Greenhouse Gardening for Fun: A Handbook. New York: Brooklyn Botanic Garden Record, 1963.

Heriteau, Jacqueline, *How to Grow and Cook It Book of Vegetables, Herbs, Fruits, and Nuts.* New York: Hawthorn, 1970.

Home Canning. Menlo Park, Calif.: Lane, 1975.

In a Pickle or in a Jam. Des Moines, Iowa: Better Homes and Gardens, 1971.

Kraft, Ken and Pat, *Home Garden Cookbook*. Garden City, N.Y.: Doubleday, 1974.

Kramer, Jack, *The Kitchen Garden Book*. New York: Bantam, 1975.

Kramer, Jack, *Your Homemade Greenhouse and How to Build It*. New York: Walker, 1975.

Kranz, Frederick H. and Jacqueline L., *Gardening Indoors Under Lights*. New York: Viking, 1975.

Langer, Richard W., *The After-Dinner Gardening Book*. New York: Collier, 1971.

Lee, Gary, *The Chinese Vegetarian Cookbook*. Concord, Calif.: Nitty Gritty, 1972.

McDonald, Elvin, *The Complete Book of Gardening Under Lights*. Garden City, N.Y.: Doubleday, 1974.

MacManiman, Gen, *Dry It, You'll Like It*. Fall City, Wash.: Livingston Food Dehydrators, 1974.

Nicholls, Richard, *The Handmade Greenhouse, from Windowsill to Backyard*. Philadelphia: Running Press.

Ridley, Clifford, *How to Grow Your Own Groceries for $100 a Year*. Salt Lake City, Utah: Hawkes, 1974.

Rodale, Jerome I., and others, *Country Gardener's Cookbook*. Emmaus, Pa.:Rodale.

Schuler, Stanley, *Gardens Are for Eating*. New York: Macmillan, 1971.

U.S. Department of Agriculture, *Complete Guide to Home Canning*. New York: Dover, 1973.

Westcott, Cynthia, *The Gardener's Bugbook*. Garden City, N.Y.: Doubleday, 1973.

Annual. Plant that completes its life cycle in one growing season.

Artificial light. Light produced by fluorescent tubes or in combination with incandescent bulbs that is utilized in growing plants.

Blanch. To bleach (a growing vegetable) by excluding light from it, as by drawing leaves over a cauliflower head to keep the buds white.

Bolting. Going to seed, especially prematurely. Some cool weather plants, such as head lettuce, if exposed to high temperatures (70° to 80° F.), will not form heads but will undergo premature seeding and be useless as vegetables. Young cabbage will bolt at low temperatures (50° to 55° F.).

Catch cropping. Planting quick-maturing vegetables in a plot where slow-maturing main crops have just been harvested. It may be done between plantings of main crops, or it may be done toward the end of a season, to utilize the last bit of frost-free time.

Clay. Soil composed of fine particles that tend to compact; it is plastic when wet but hard when dry. It takes water slowly, holds it tightly, drains slowly, and generally restricts water and air circulation.

Common garden soil. Soil used for growing flowers and vegetables that contains organic and mineral matter.

Companion plants. Plants that influence each other, either beneficially or detrimentally. The influence may be chemical (odors or other exudates may have an effect), luminescent (a tall sun plant may protect a shade-loving low plant), etc.

Compost. Mixture of loose vegetation, manure, or other once-living wastes that is left to decay through bacterial action and that is used for fertilizing and soil conditioning. Ripe compost is compost that has completed its decomposition and is ready for use.

Cotyledon. Food storage parts of the plant that are pushed out of the ground before the leaves.

Crop stretching. Any mode of vegetable planting that efficiently extends the use of a plot of ground. It may involve intercropping, succession cropping, or catch cropping, or it may involve the use of trellises, poles, or other devices to train plants in the air to save ground space.

Crown. Section of a plant at which stem and foot merge.

Cutting. Section of a stem or root that is cut off and planted in a rooting medium (such as vermiculite or soil) so that it will sprout roots and develop into a plant that is similar in every respect to the parent plant. Nurseries sell powdered "rooting hormone" that encourages root growth for this purpose (directions for use are given on the package).

Dormant. Passing through a seasonal period of no active growth. Most perennials and other plants go dormant during the winter.

Fish emulsion. Liquid mixture containing discarded soluble fish parts, used as fertilizer. It contains usually 5 to 10 percent nitrogen and lesser amounts of phosphorus and potassium.

Flat. Shallow box in which seeds are planted to produce seedlings, generally indoors.

Foot-candle. Unit of illumination used to determine the quantity of light at any one place.

Frond. Leaf of a fern or palm; also, any fernlike leaf.

Germination. Sprouting of a new plant from seed.

Hardening (usually with *off*). Getting an indoor-grown seedling used to outdoor weather by exposing it gradually to the outdoors.

Heavy feeder. Any vegetable that absorbs large amounts of soil nutrients in the process of growth. Heavy feeders include cabbage, cauliflower, corn, cucumbers, leafy vegetables, rhubarb, and tomatoes.

Hot cap. Small waxed-paper cone that is set over an individual young plant to

Glossary

protect it from springtime cold. It is commercially made, one brand being called Hotkap.

Humus. Black or brown decayed plant and animal matter that forms the organic part of soil.

Intercropping. Also called *interplanting*, planting quick-maturing and slow-maturing vegetables close together and then harvesting the quick-maturing ones before the slow-maturing ones have become big enough to overshadow or outcrowd them. Quick-maturing lettuce, for instance, can be seeded between beans.

Leaching. Dissolving nutrients or salts out of soil or fertilizer by the action of water percolating downward.

Legume. Plant or fruit of a plant that bears edible pods, such as beans and peas. Legumes restore fertility to a soil by taking nitrogen compounds from the air and making them available in the soil.

Light feeder. Any vegetable that requires small or moderate amounts of nutrients in the process of growth. Root crops are light feeders.

Mulch. Protective covering placed over the soil between plants. It may be peat moss, sawdust, compost, paper, opaque plastic sheeting, etc. Its purpose is to reduce evaporation, maintain even soil temperature, reduce erosion, and inhibit the sprouting of weeds.

Nanometer. Scientific unit for measuring light waves.

Nematode. Microscopic parasitic worm that infects plants and animals (phylum *Nematoda*).

Nitrogen. One of three most important plant nutrients, the others being phosphorus and potassium. It is particularly essential in the production of leaves and stems. An excess of nitrogen can produce abundant foliage and few flowers and fruit.

Nutrient. Any of the sixteen elements that, in usable form, are absorbed by plants as nourishment. Plants obtain carbon, hydrogen, and oxygen from water and air, and the other elements from the soil. The main soil elements are nitrogen, phosphorus, and potassium; the trace elements are boron, calcium, chlorine, copper, iron, manganese, magnesium, molybdenum, sulfur, and zinc.

Organic. Deriving from living organisms, either plants or animals. In gardening, it denotes fertilizers or sprays of plant or animal origin, as opposed to those employing synthetic chemicals.

Peat. Prehistoric plant remains that have decayed under airless conditions beneath standing water, such as a bog. Peat moss, the most common form, is the remains of sphagnum moss. Its nutrient content is low—less than 1 percent nitrogen and less than 0.1 percent phosphorus and potassium; it is also highly acid. Added to the soil, it makes soil finer and more water-absorbent, but will also increase its acidity.

Peat pellet. Small net-enclosed peat wafer that rises to six or seven times its original size on the addition of water. When expanded, it takes seeds, which develop into seedlings. Pellet and seedling together can be sown in the garden.

Peat pot. Tiny molded container made of peat, usually containing its own soil or planting medium. Seeds are planted in the pot, and seedling and pot together are transplanted to the soil outdoors. Pot shapes vary from cubes to truncated cones or pyramids.

Perennial. Plant that continues living over a number of years. It may die down to the roots at the end of each season but shoots up afresh every year. In areas of mild winters, the foliage may remain all year.

Phosphorus. One of the three most important plant nutrients, the others being nitrogen and potassium. It is especially associated with the production of seeds and fruits and with the development of good roots.

Pinching. Snipping off or shortening (shoots or buds) in order to produce a certain plant shape or to increase or decrease blooms or fruits. The snipping is done with finger and thumb. Pinching the terminus of the main stem forces greater side branching. Pinching off the side shoots, conversely, stimulates more growth in the main stem, as well as in other remaining side stems.

Pollination. Sexual reproduction in plants. Pollen, the fine dust produced by the male stamen of a flower, joins with the ovule of the female pistil of a flower, and the result is a seed to produce the next generation.

Potash. Any potassium or potassium compound used for fertilizer. The potash in wood ash is potassium carbonate.

Potassium. One of the three most important plant nutrients, the others being nitrogen and phosphorus. Its special value is to promote the general vigor of a plant and to increase its resistance to disease and cold. It also promotes sturdy roots.

Potting mix (planting mix). Prepared mix for growing plants sold at most garden stores. Most contain a wood product, sand, vermiculite, fertilizer, and lime.

Pyrethrum. Insecticide made from the dried powdered flowers of certain plants of the *Chrysanthemum* genus. It is especially effective against sphids, leaf hoppers, caterpillars, thrips, and leaf miners.

Rotenone. Insecticide derived from the roots (and sometimes the stems) of certain New World tropical shrubs and vines of the genera *Derris* and *Lonchocarpus*. It is especially effective against beetles, caterpillars, leaf miners, thrips, aphids, and leaf hoppers.

Ryania. Insecticide made from the ground stems of a tropical South American shrub, *Patrisia pyrifera*. It is used especially against the corn borer.

Sand. Tiny, water-worn particles of silicon and other rocks, each usually less than 2 millimeters in diameter. The granules allow free movement of air and water—so free, however, that water flows out readily and leaches out nutrients quickly.

Seedling. Very young plant, especially one grown from seed.

Set. *1* small bulb, tuber, or root, or a section of a bulb, tuber, or root that is planted; *2* as a verb, often with *out*, to fix (a plant) in the soil, as in *to set out seedlings.*

Soil Aeration. Flow of oxygen and carbon dioxide within the soil, between the ground surface and plant roots and soil microorganisms. Plant roots absorb oxygen and release carbon dioxide (as opposed to plant leaves, which absorb carbon dioxide and release oxygen). Oxygen is also necessary to soil bacteria and fungi to decompose organic matter and produce humus.

Succession Planting. Planting a new crop as soon as the first one is harvested. This harvesting and replanting in the same spot may occur more than once in a season, and it may involve the planting of the same vegetable or of different vegetables.

Thinning. Pulling up young plants from a group so that the ones that are left in the soil have more room to develop properly.

Vegetable Classification. Categorization of vegetables on the basis of the part of the plant that is used for food. Major root vegetables are beets, carrots, radishes, turnips and rutabagas. A common stem vegetable is asparagus. Major tuber vegetables are potatoes and yams. Major leaf and leafstalk vegetables are Brussels sprouts, cabbage, celery, endive, kale, lettuce, mustard greens, rhubarb, spinach, and Swiss chard. Major bulb vegetables are onions and garlic. The chief immature flowering vegetables are broccoli and cauliflower. Major vegetables that come as fruits (the seed-bearing parts) are beans, corn, cucumbers, eggplant, melons, okra, peas, peppers, squash, and tomatoes.

Vermiculite. Artificial planting medium consisting of inflated mica. It is highly water-absorbent and light-weight and is used mainly for growing seeds or plant cuttings. It can also be used to increase the water absorbency of soils.

Index